LETTER TRACING
PRACTICE

This book belongs to:

_____

_____

B.C. Lester Books
Geography publications for the people since 2019.

Visit us at www.bclesterbooks.com for more!

Outside the exemption notices above covering personal and educational use, no part of this book may be copied, reproduced or sold without the express permission from the copyright owner.

Copyright B.C. Lester Books 2021. All rights reserved.

A MESSAGE FROM THE PUBLISHER...

Hey! Thank you for making the purchase, we really hope you enjoy this book. If you have the chance, then all feedback is greatly appreciated. We have put a lot of effort into making this book, so if you are not completely satisfied, please email us at ben@bclesterbooks.com and we will do our best to address the issues. If you have any suggestions, enquries or want to send us a selfie with this book, then email at the same address - ben@bclesterbooks.com

Is this book misprinted? Drop us an email with a photo of the misprint and we will send out another copy!

WHO ARE WE AT B.C LESTER BOOKS?

B.C. Lester Books is a publishing firm based in Buckinghamshire, UK. With our passion and how-know for geography, we aim to provide quality works based around the topic. We have already released a selection of activity, trivia and fact books for kids and adults and are working hard to bring you wider selection. Have a suggestion for us? Then drop us an email! We are all ears!

ARE YOU A TEACHER, PARENT OR CARING FOR CHILDREN?

✓ We have you covered. You may **copy** and **reproduce** any part of this book in **any amount** for personal and educational purposes.

SOME OF OUR OTHER TITLES YOU MAY LIKE!

Are you looking for a challenge for your children? Test their knowledge of the world with this fun, colorful quiz book!

Enjoy coloring and geography?

Colorful flags handbook for kids.

CONTENTS

Features & How To Use This Book..4
Letter Guides & Letter Tracing A-Z...5
Word Tracing...83
Sentence Tracing...102
Empty Handwriting Sheets...115

Hello! Our names are Sam and Lucy and we will be guiding you as you go through this book. Look out for us for any tips and tricks!

Adventure Theme Letter Tracing Practice　　　*Introduction*

1. Step by step guides to each letter's uppercase and lowercase

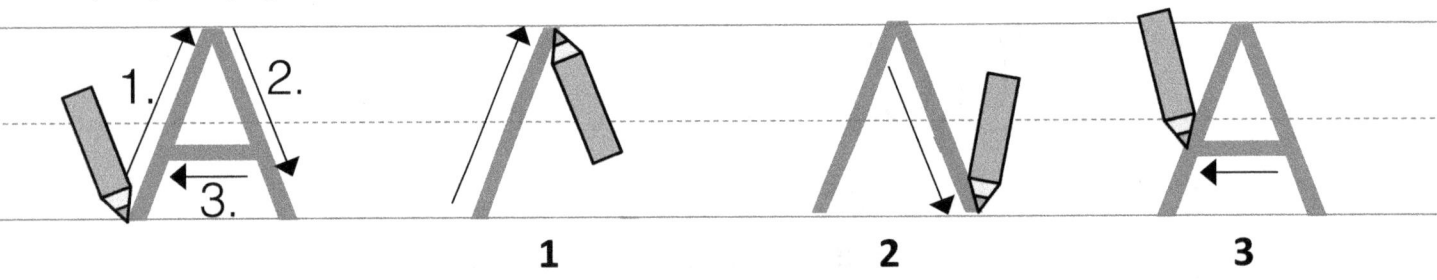

2. Letter tracing for your child to practice the correct movement.

3. A harder section where your child may try writing the letter freehand!

4. When your child is confident with the letters, then have a go at the words!

5. When your child is confident with the words, then have a go at the sentences!

6. To make the most out of this book, try cutting along the scissor line of every odd page from page 5 onwards, sticking the page in a plastic wallet and into a folder. Use a marker pen on the wallet and wipe clean after for unlimited tracing!

A is for...

Africa

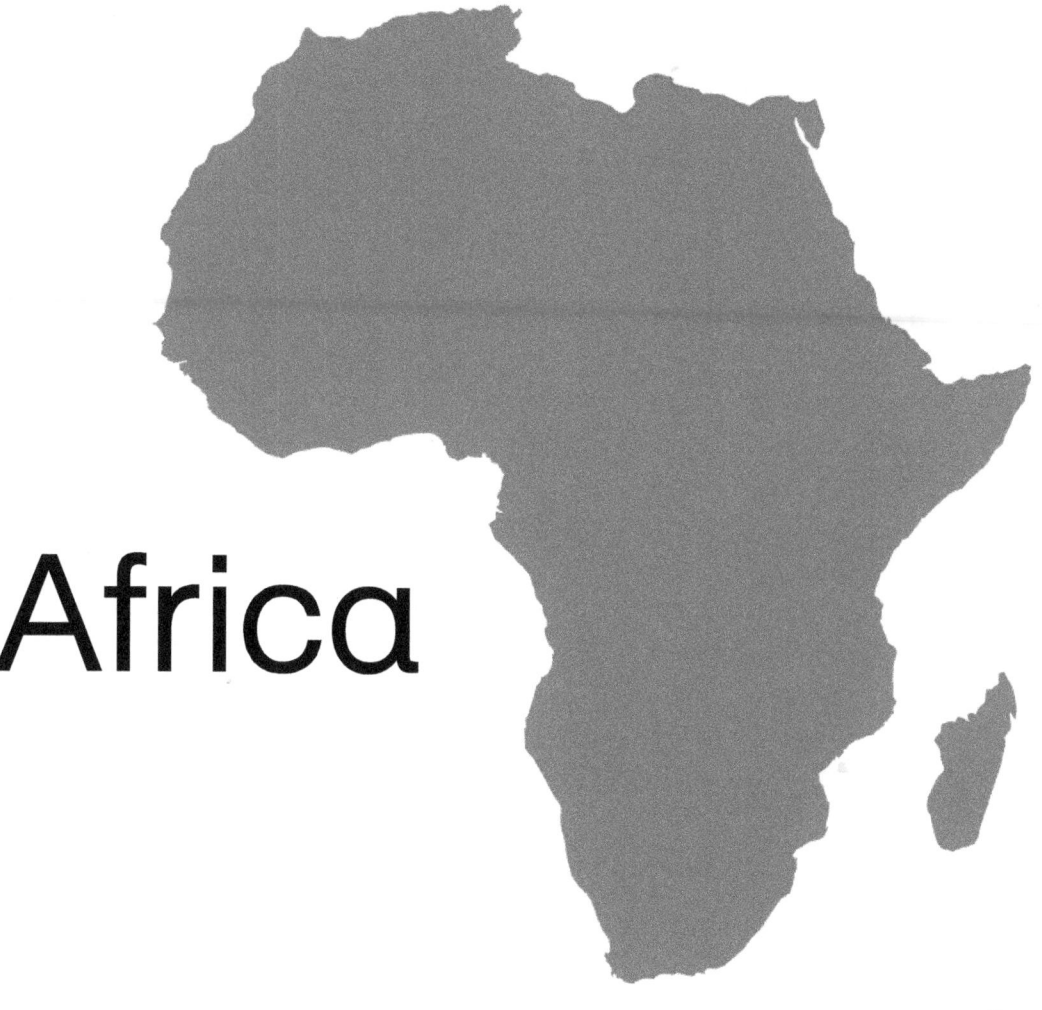

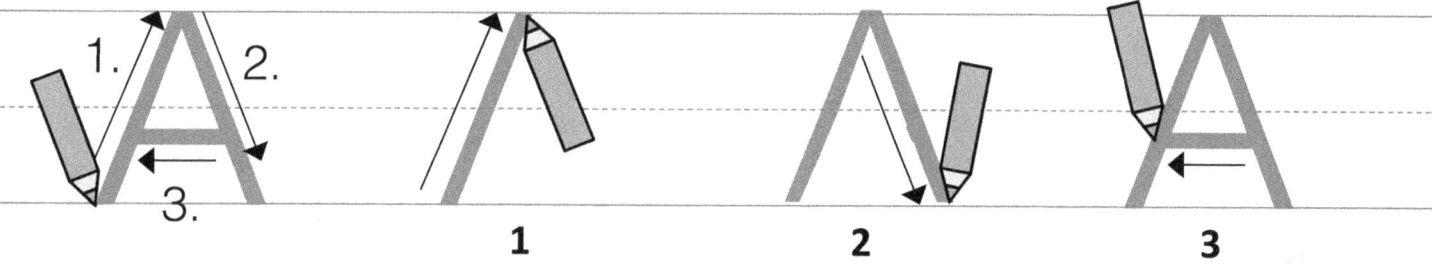

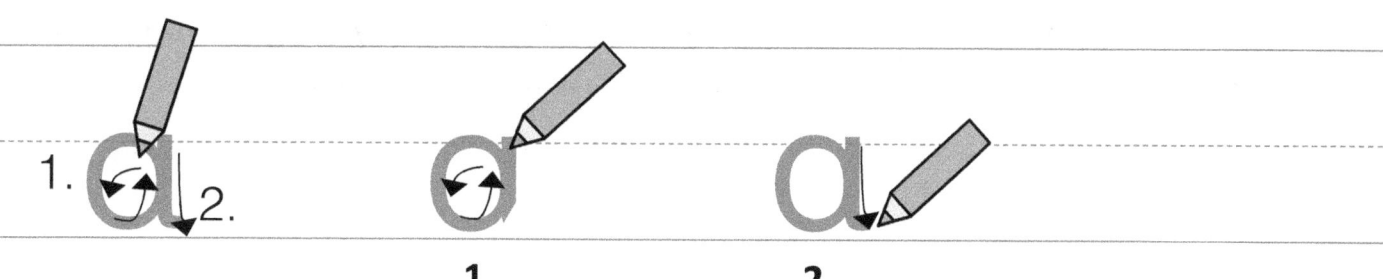

Ready for a challenge? The next page has one letter to trace, then followed by a space to you to try and write freely! Good luck!

Nice, well done. How did you find that. Flip the page for the letter B.

B is for...
Beach

B B B B

b b b b

B B B B

b b b b

C is for...
Cave

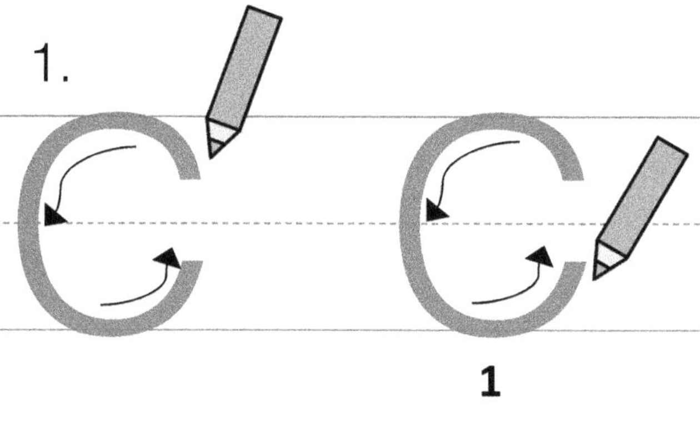

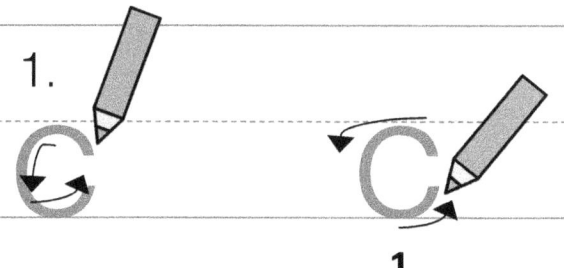

1.

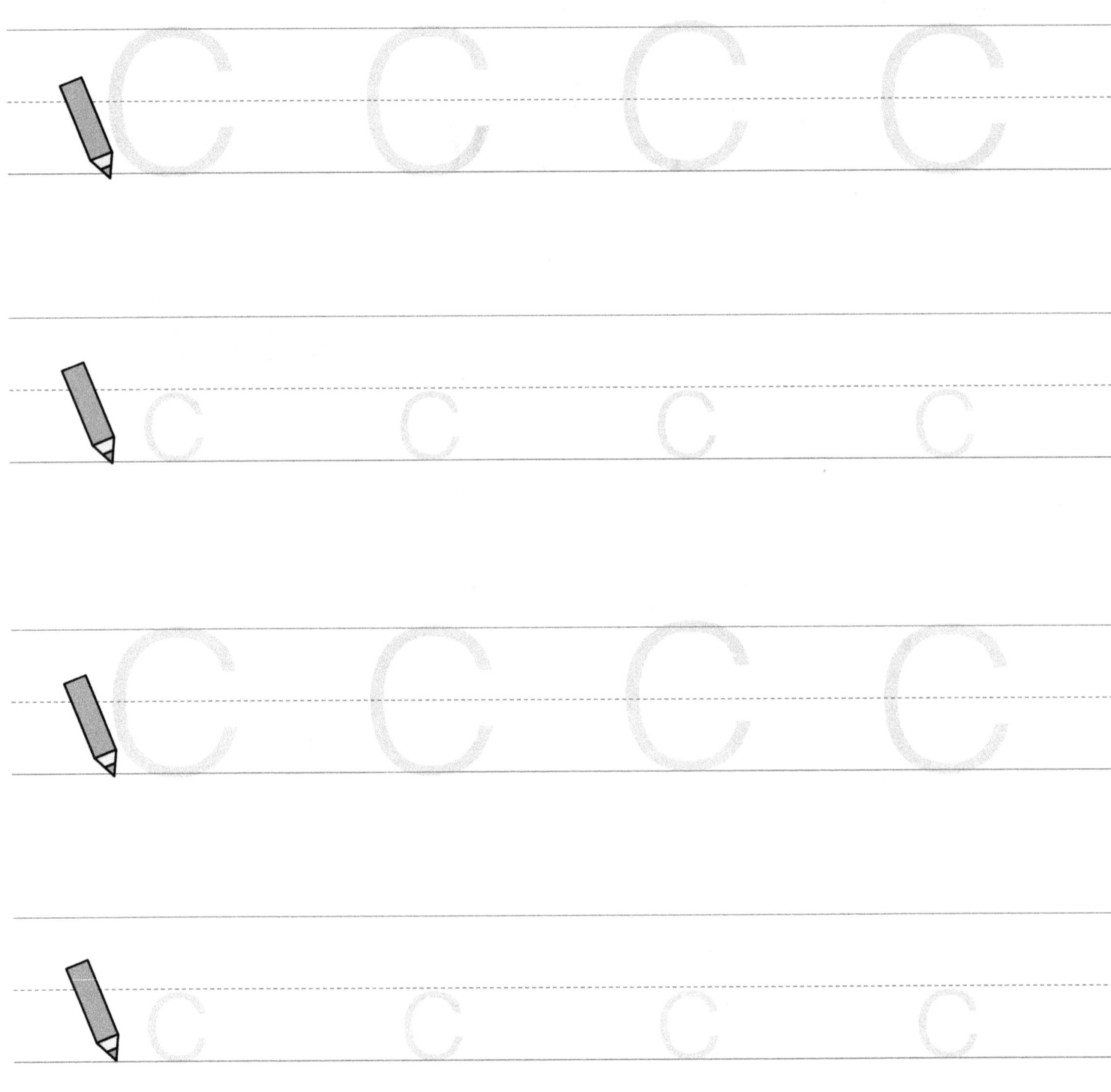

D is for...

Desert

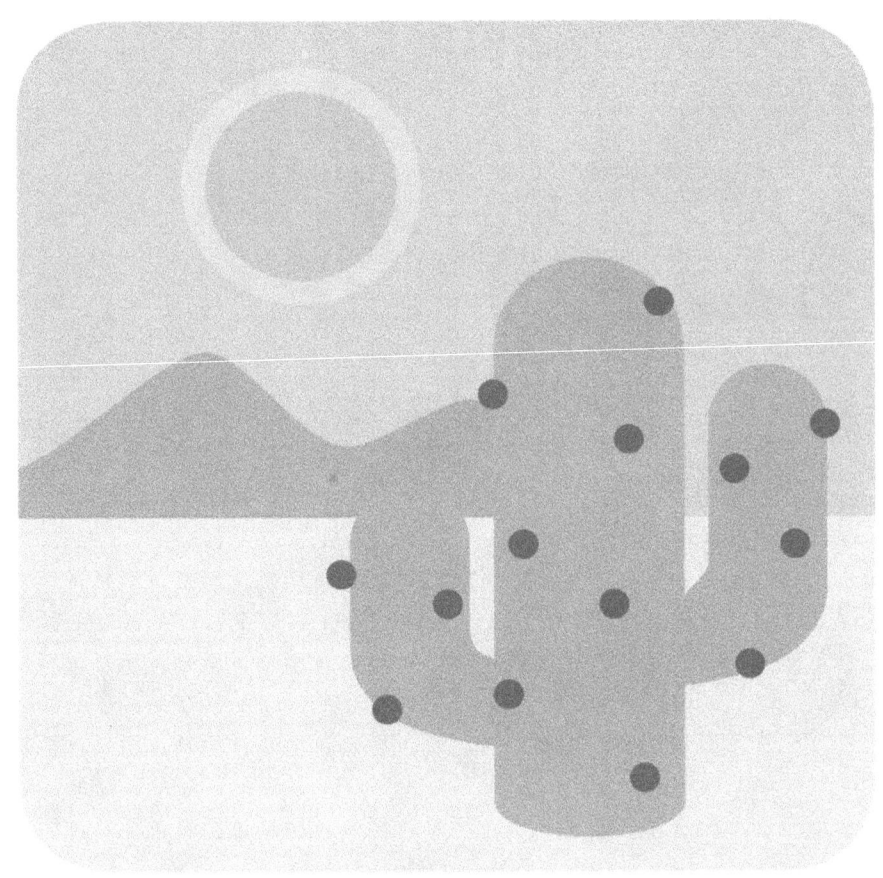

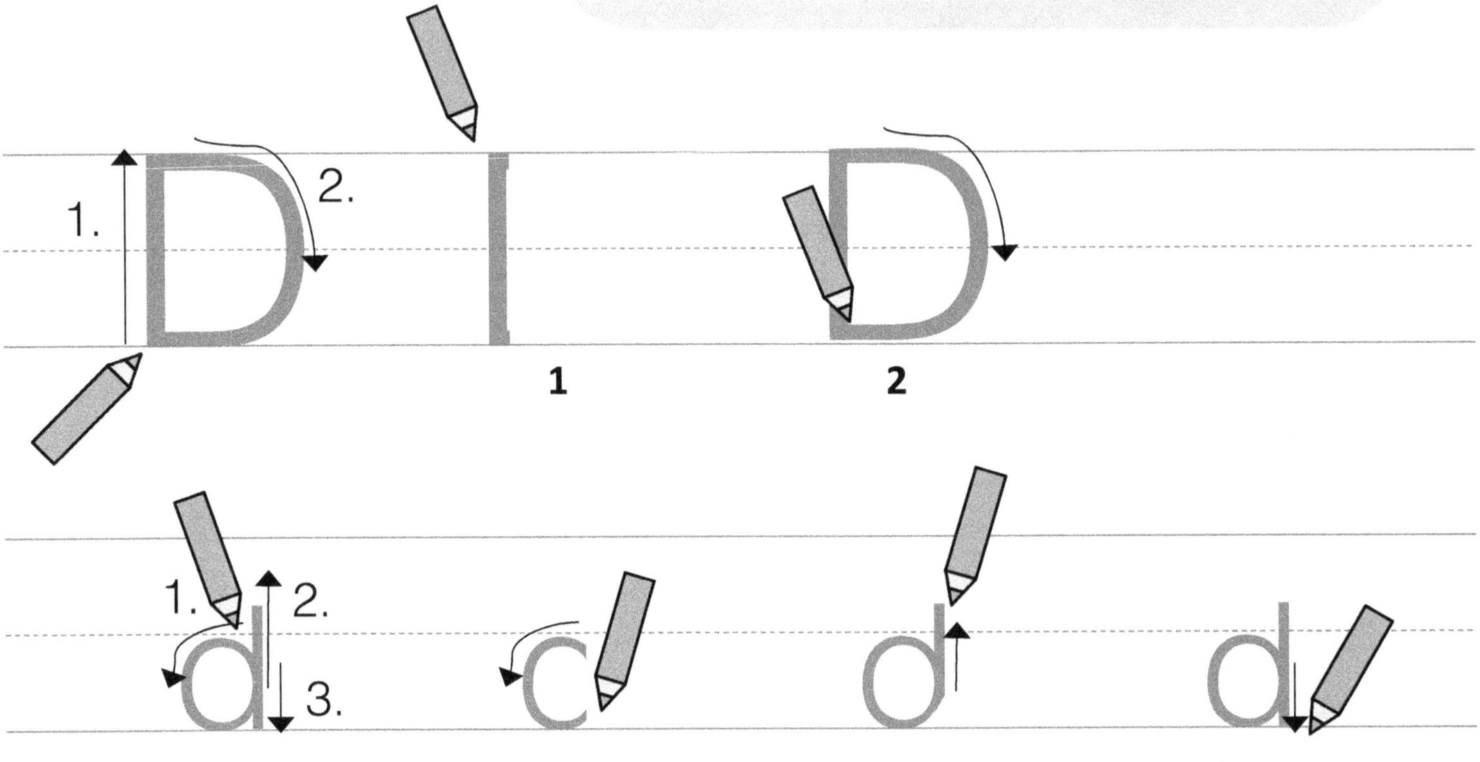

E is for...

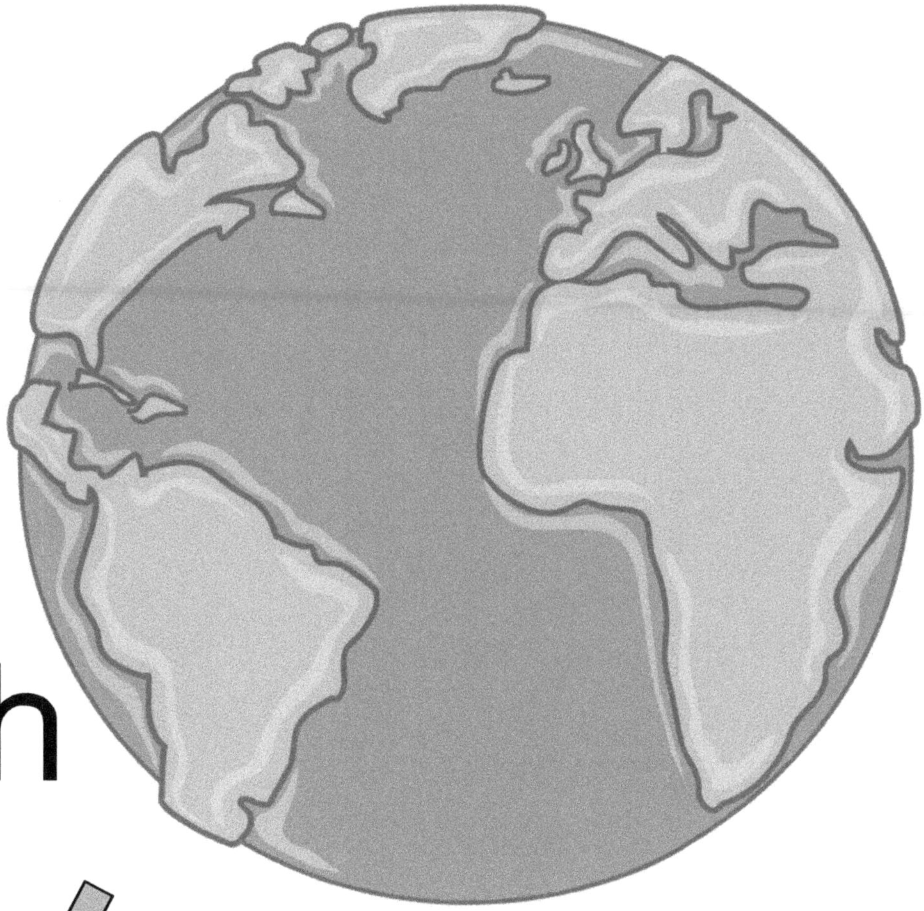

Earth

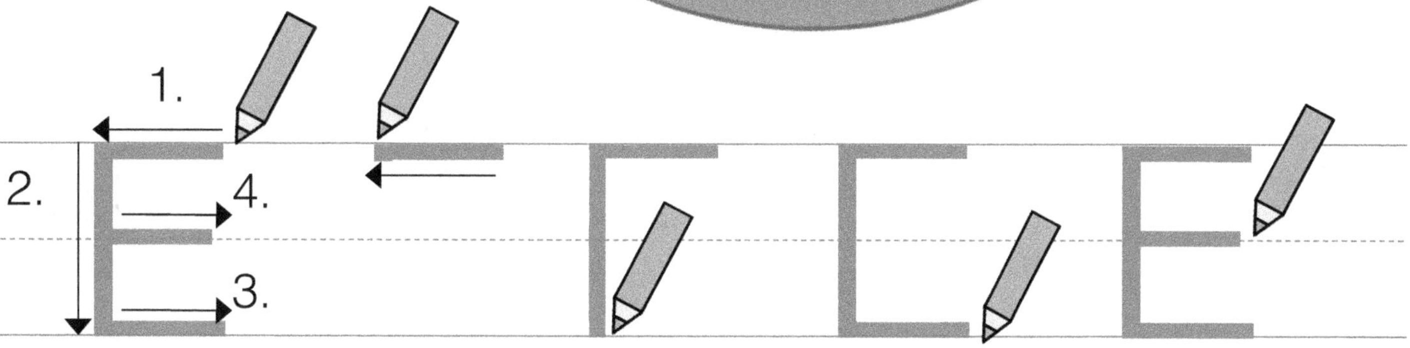

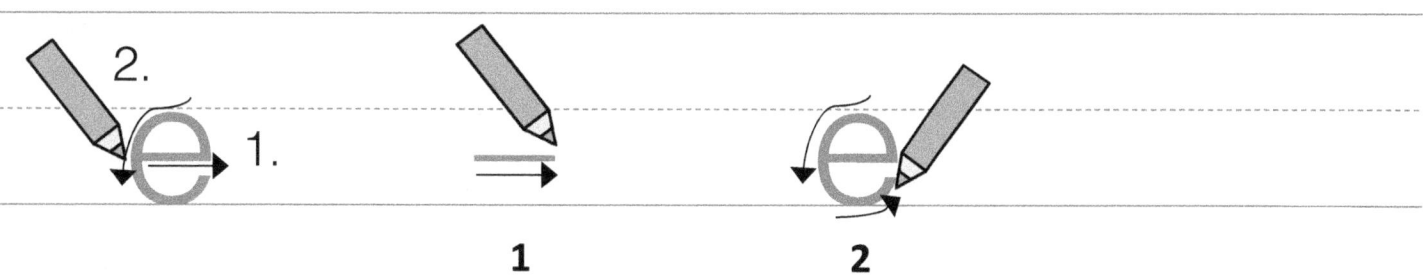

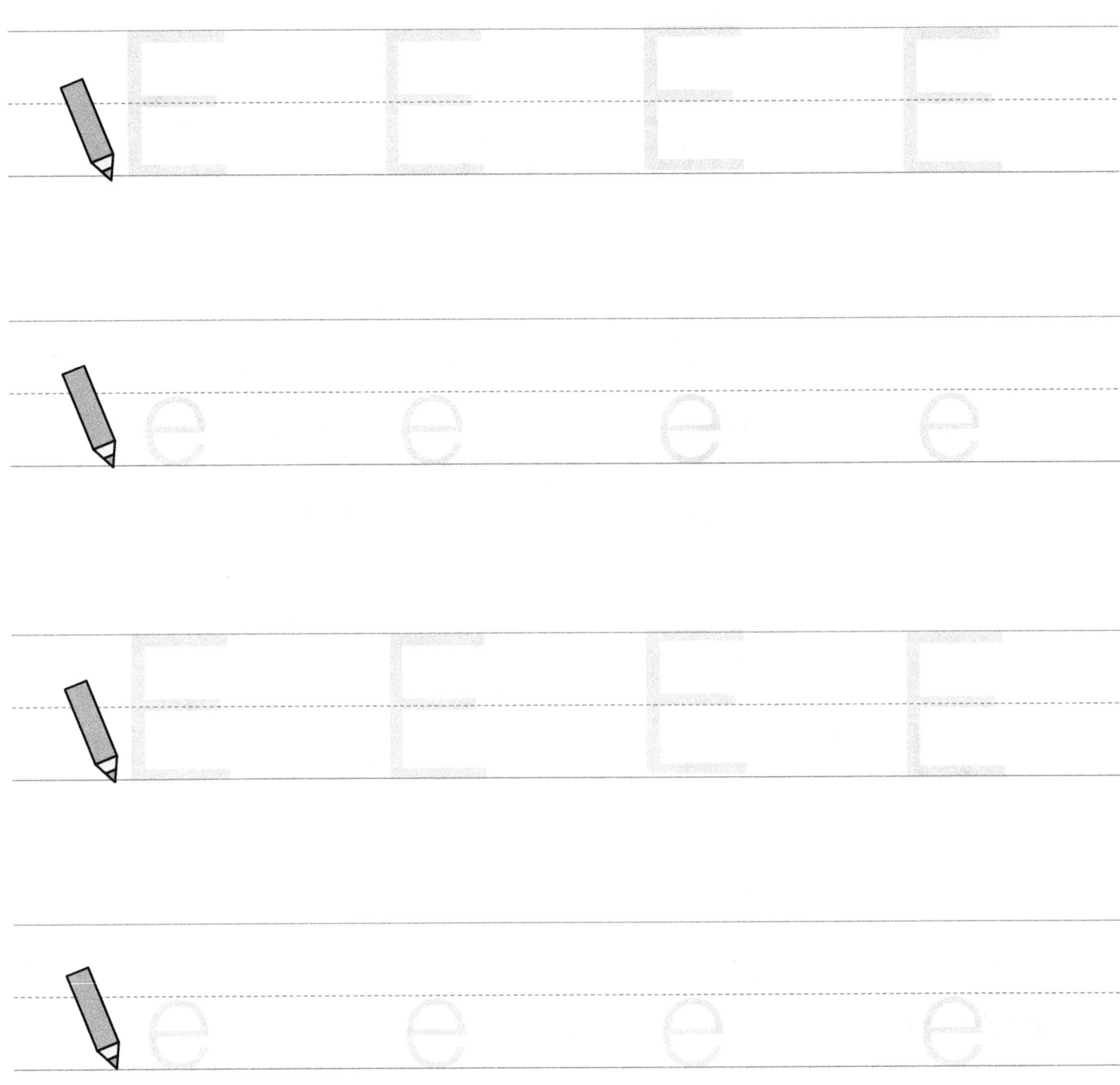

How are you getting on?

F is for...
Forest

G is for...
Grass

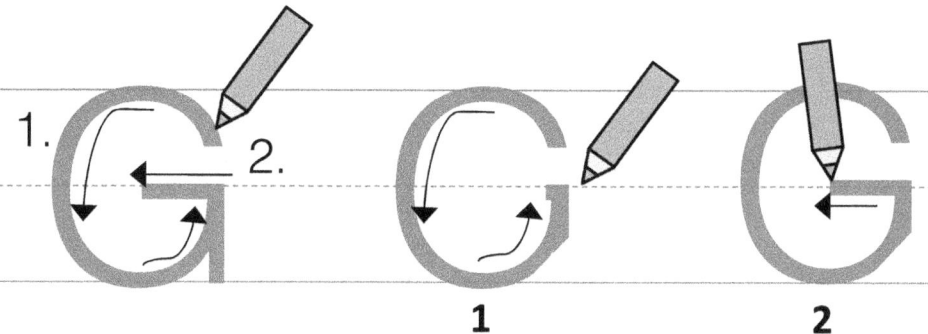

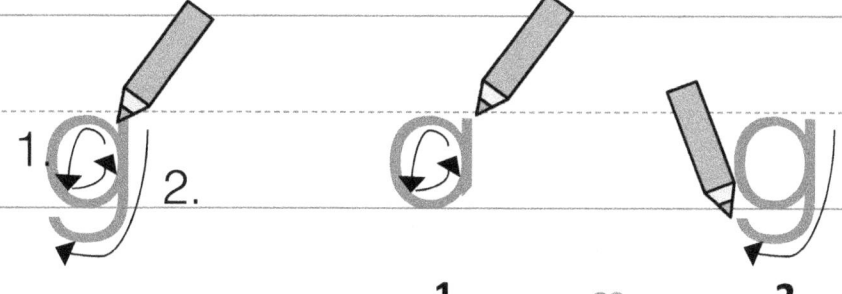

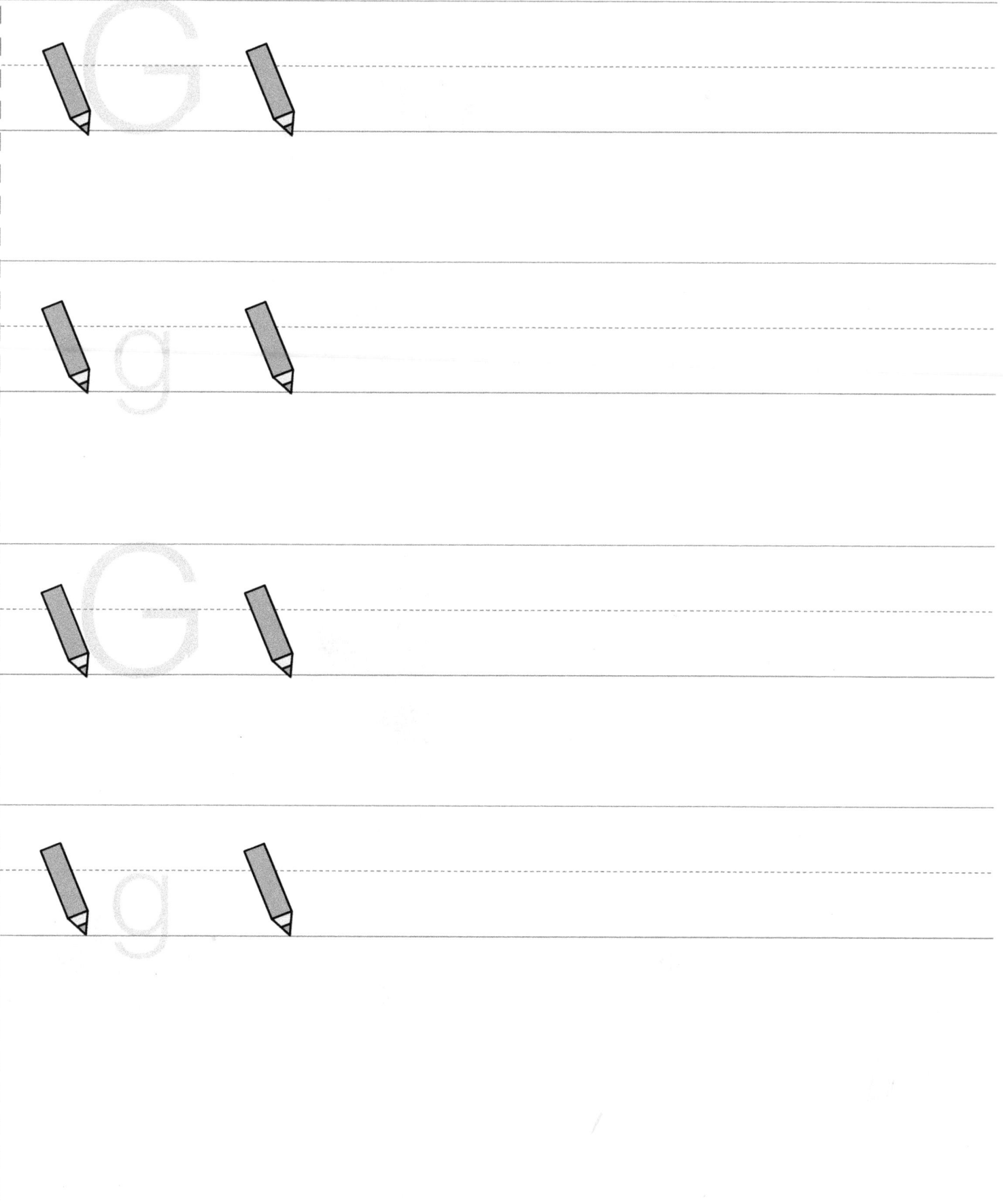

H is for...

Hut

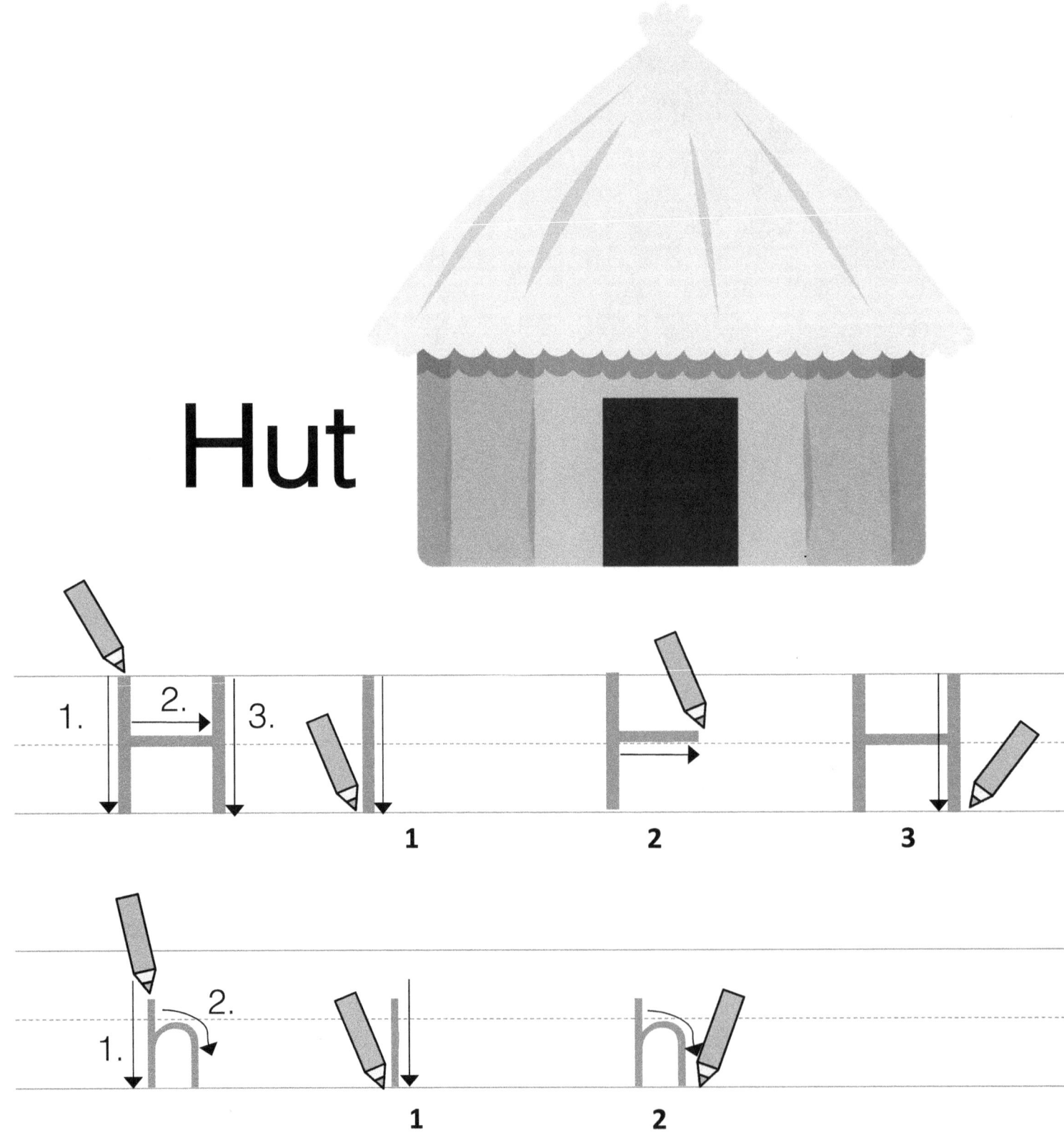

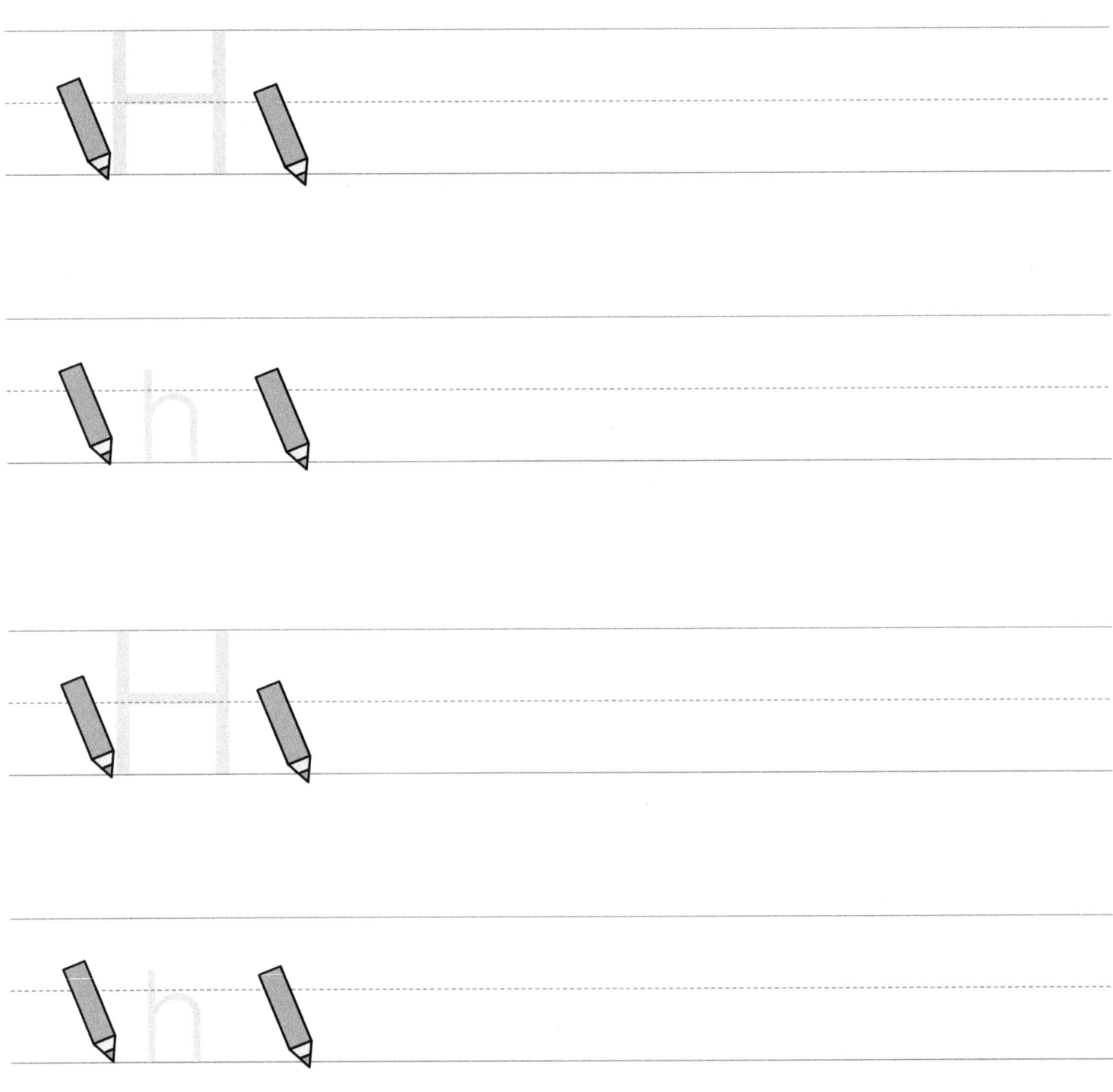

I is for...

Island

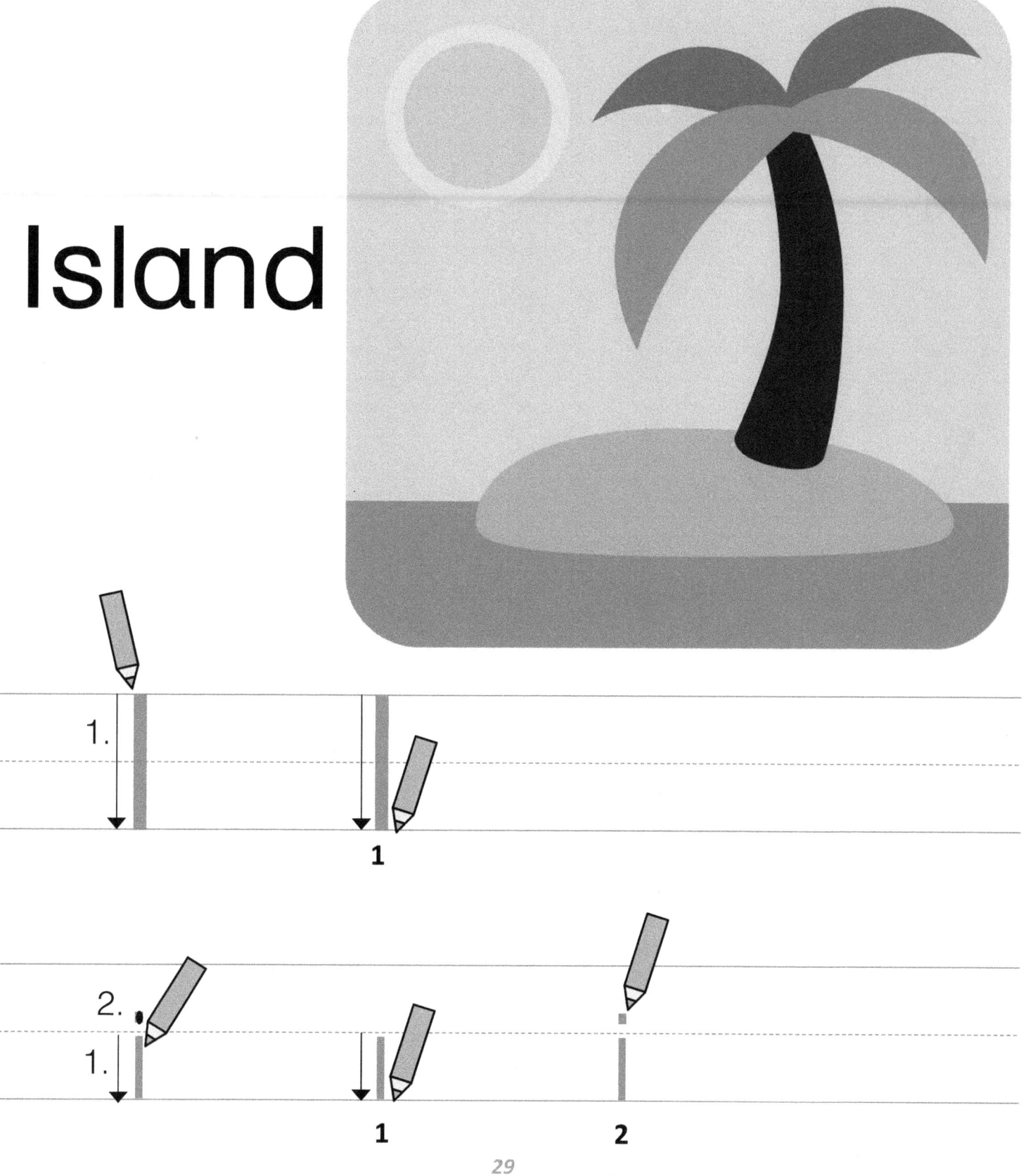

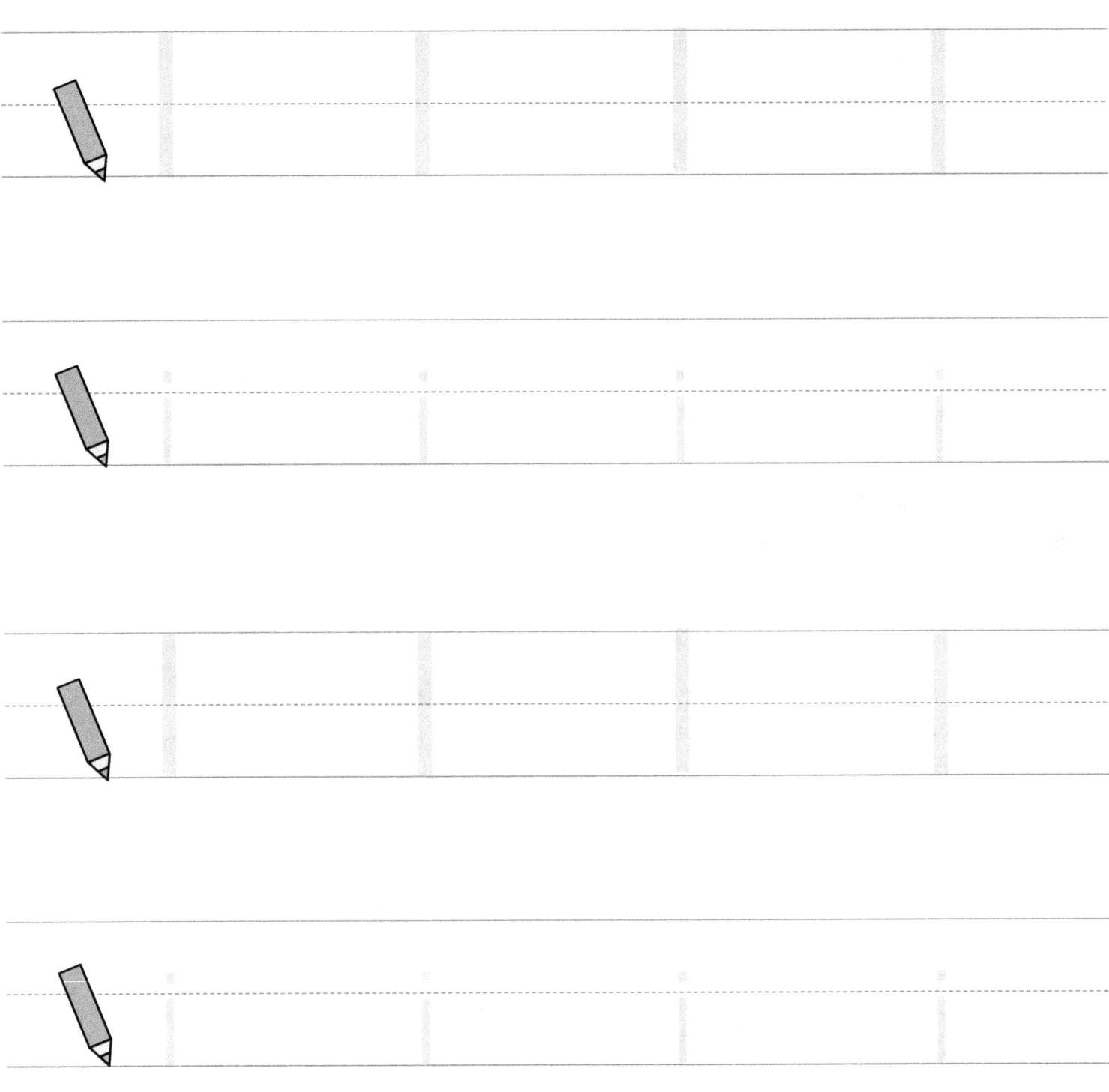

J is for...

Jungle

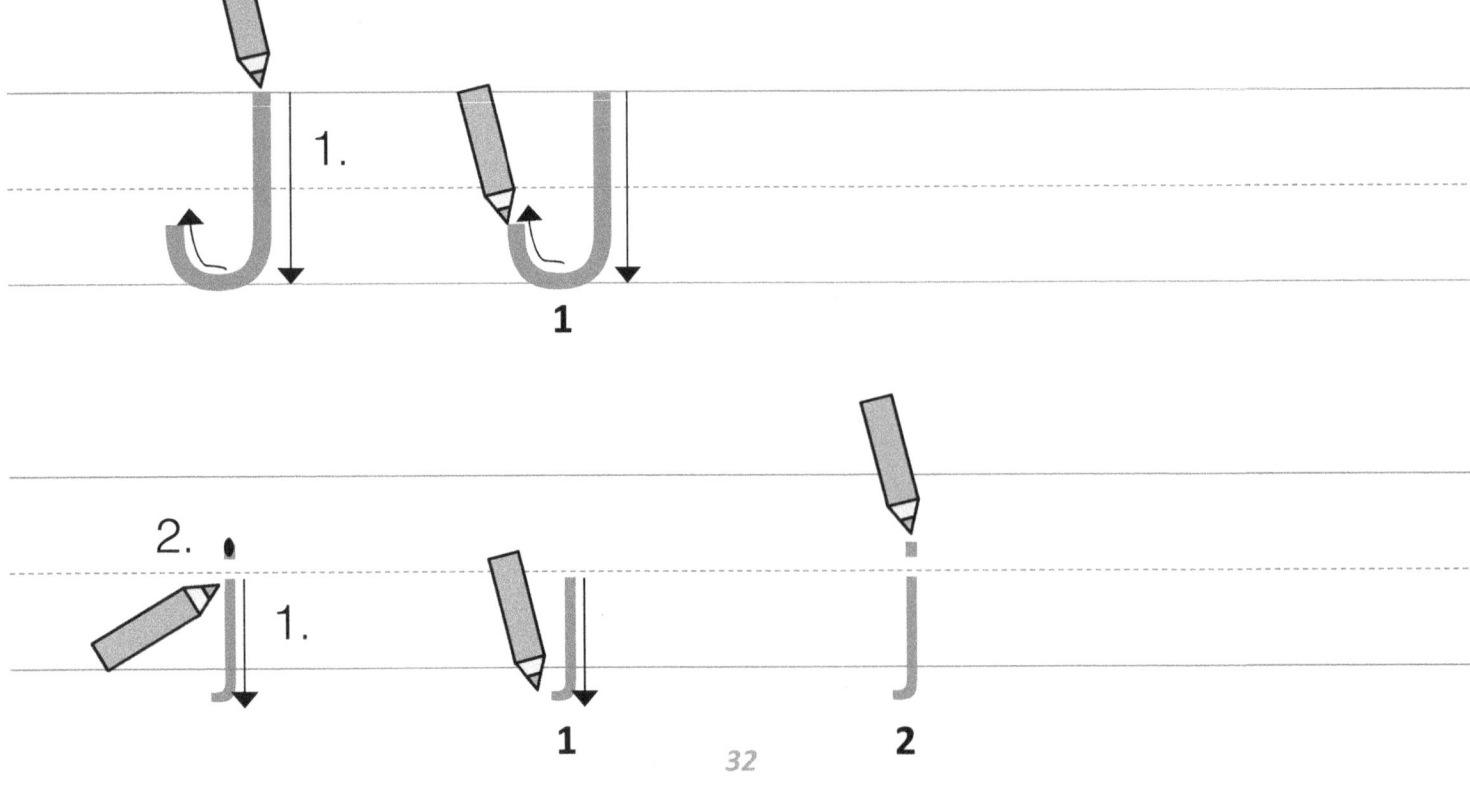

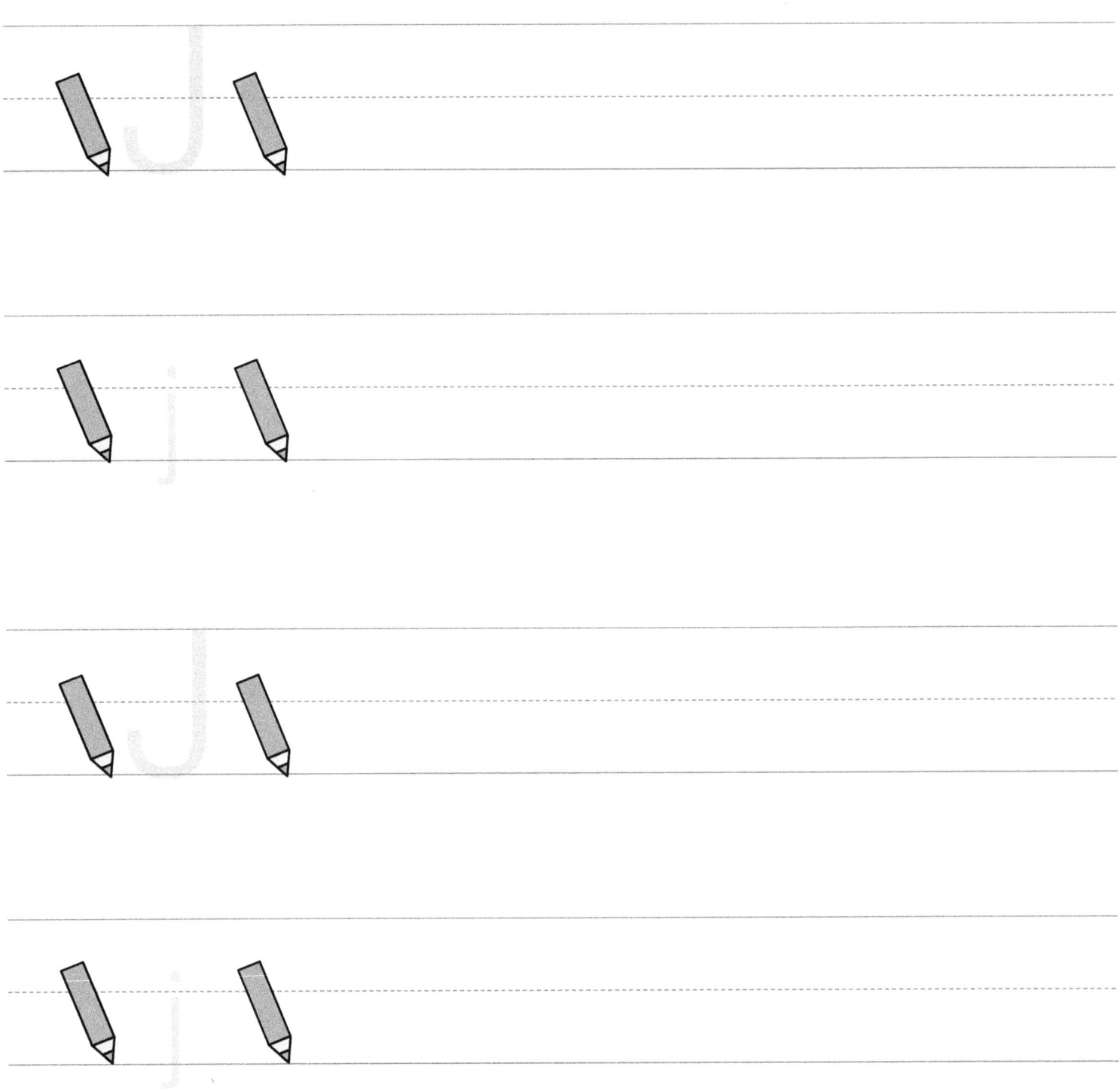

K is for...

Kangaroo

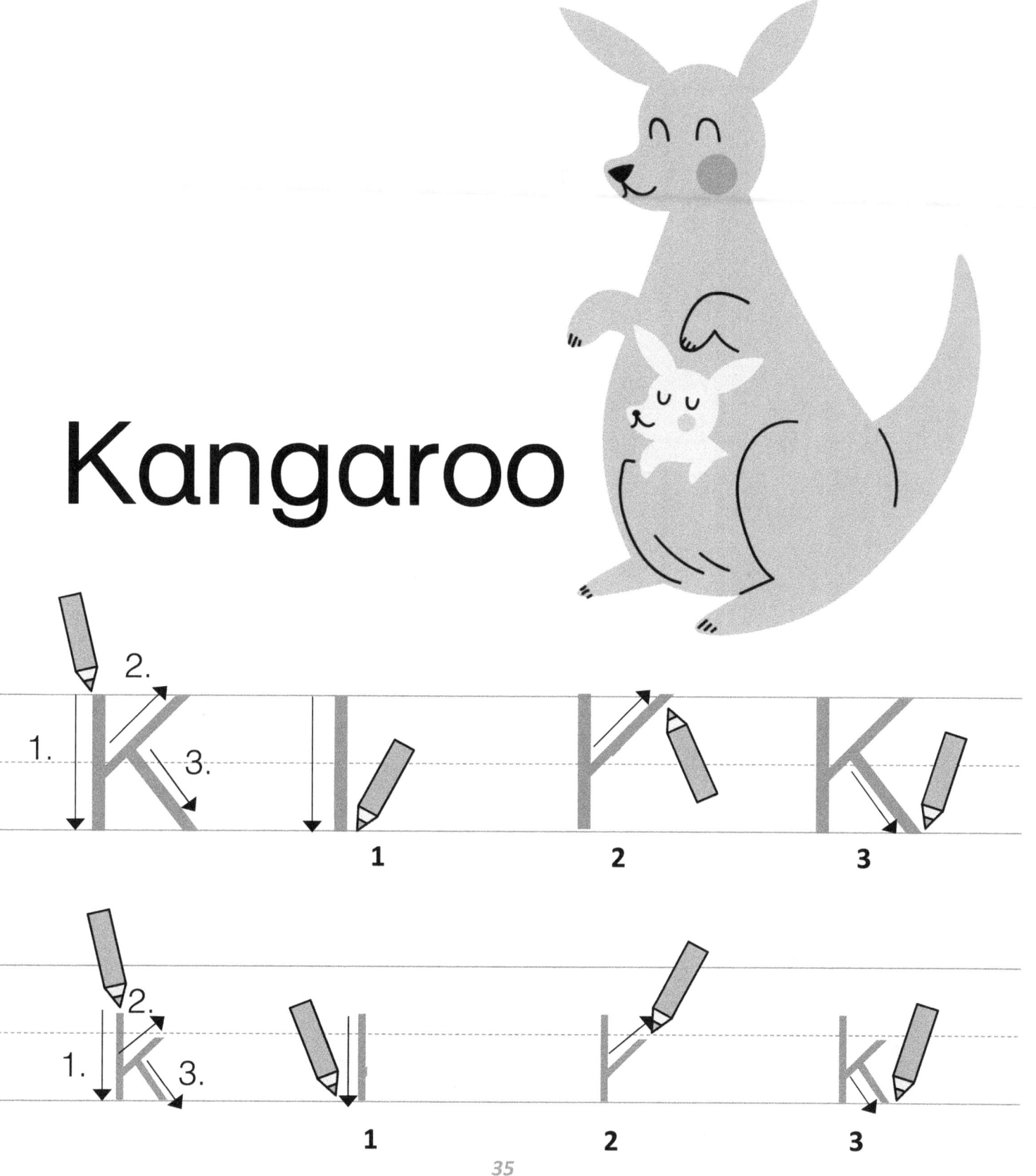

L is for...
Lake

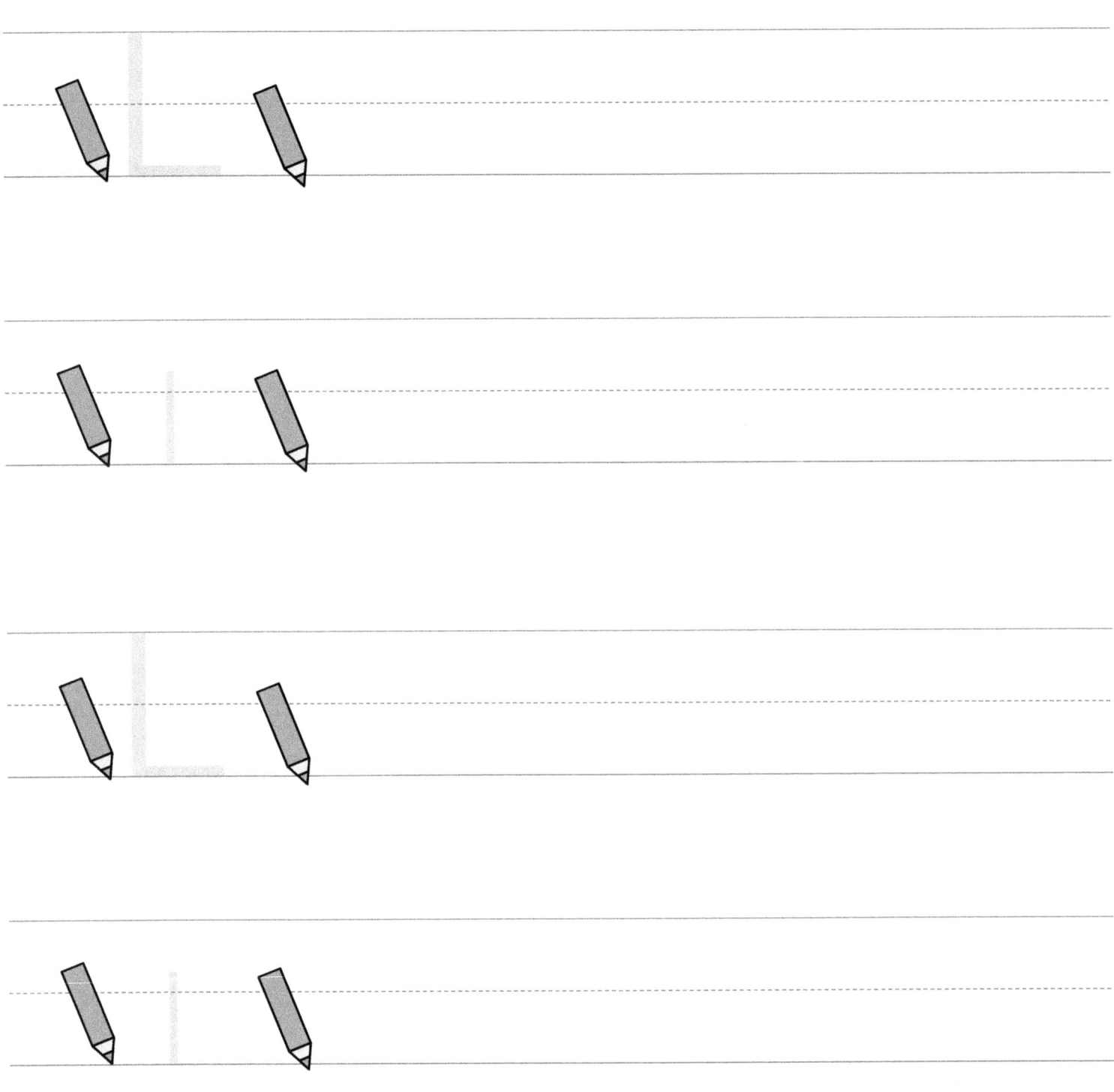

M is for...

Mountain

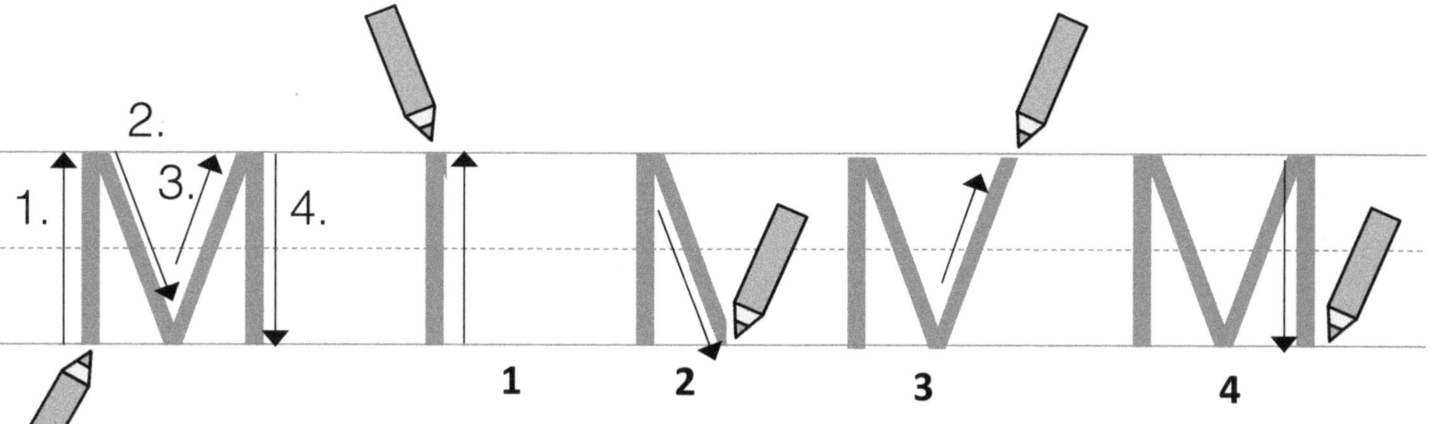

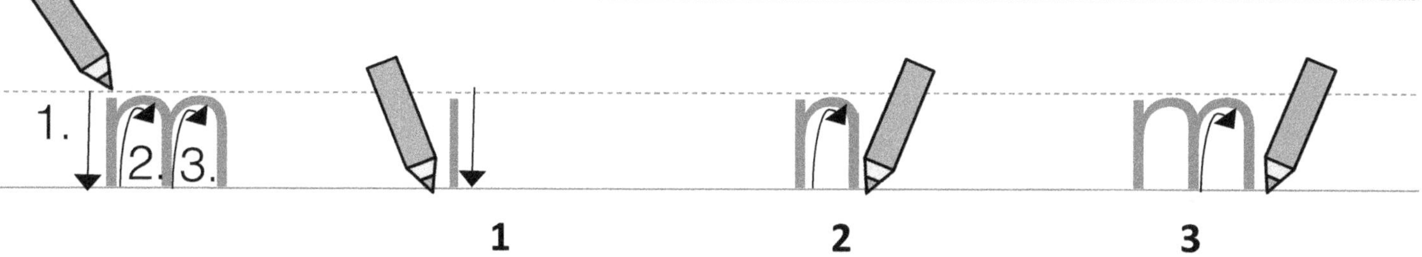

N is for...

Nature

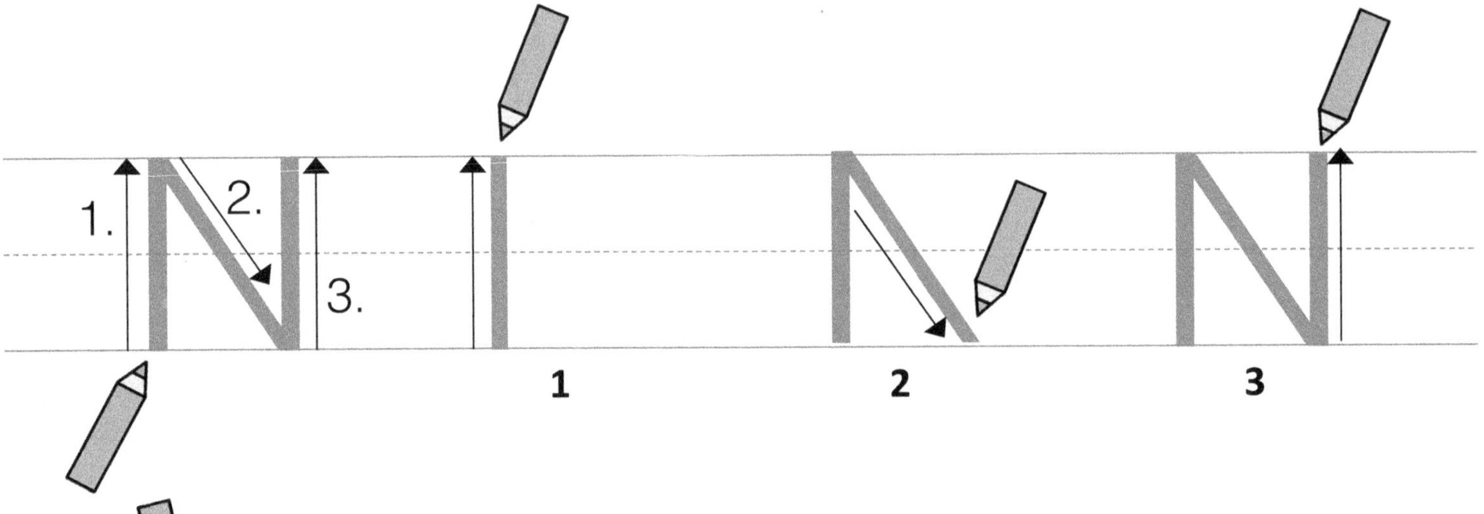

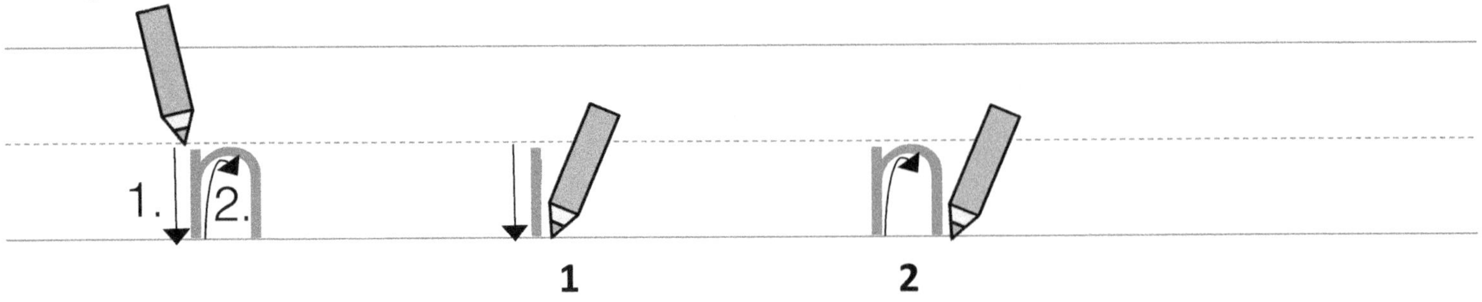

O is for...
Ocean

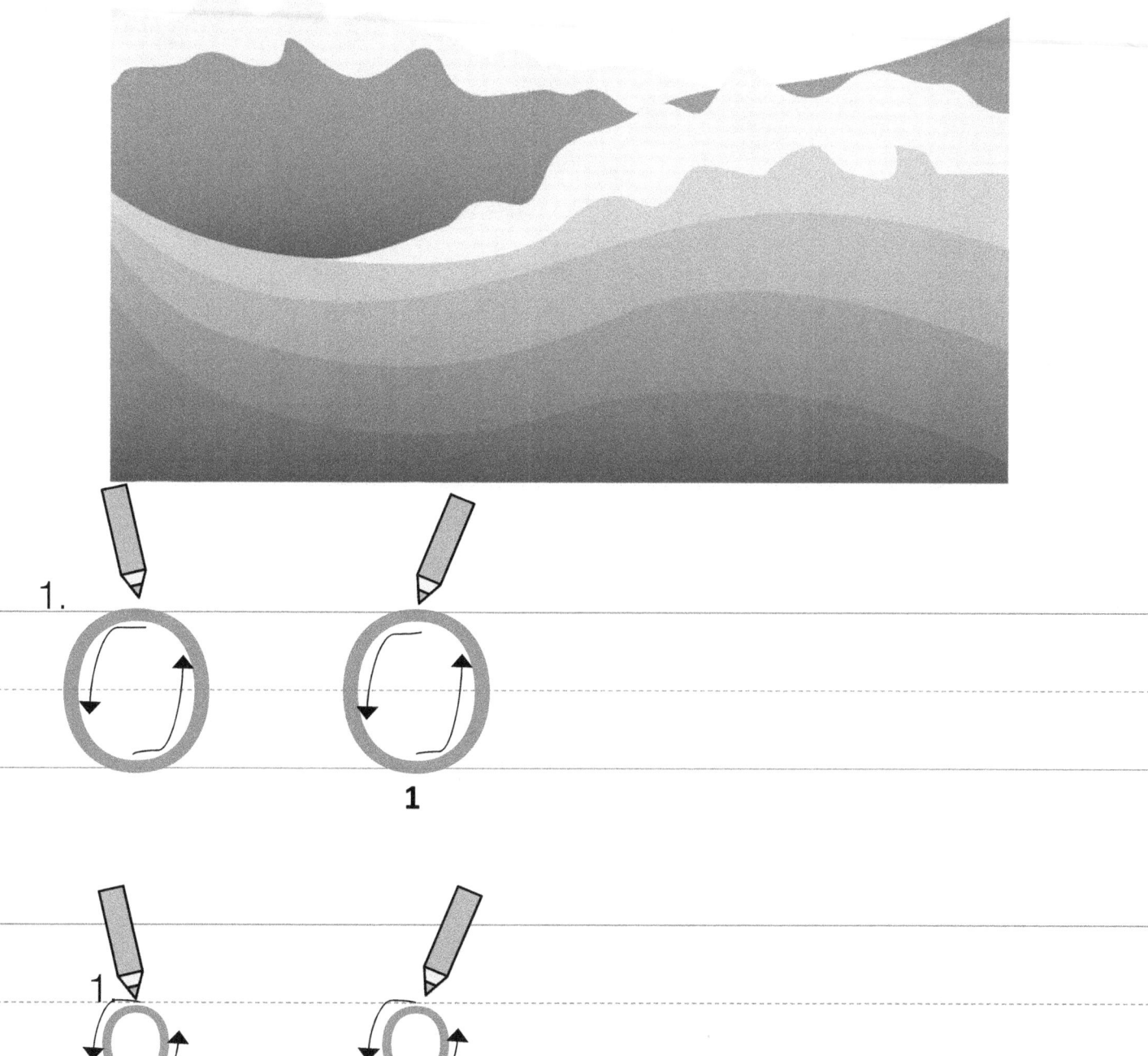

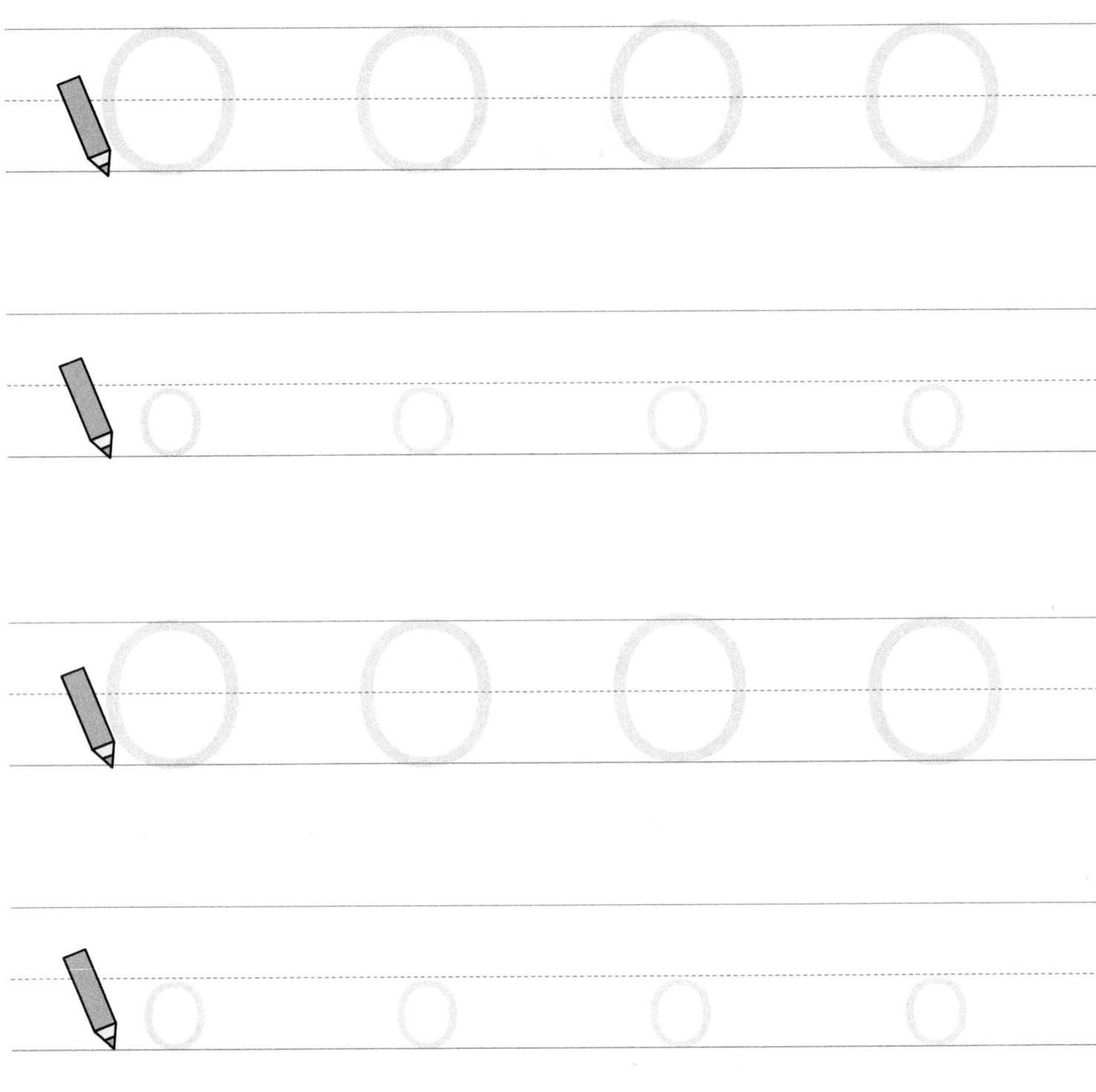

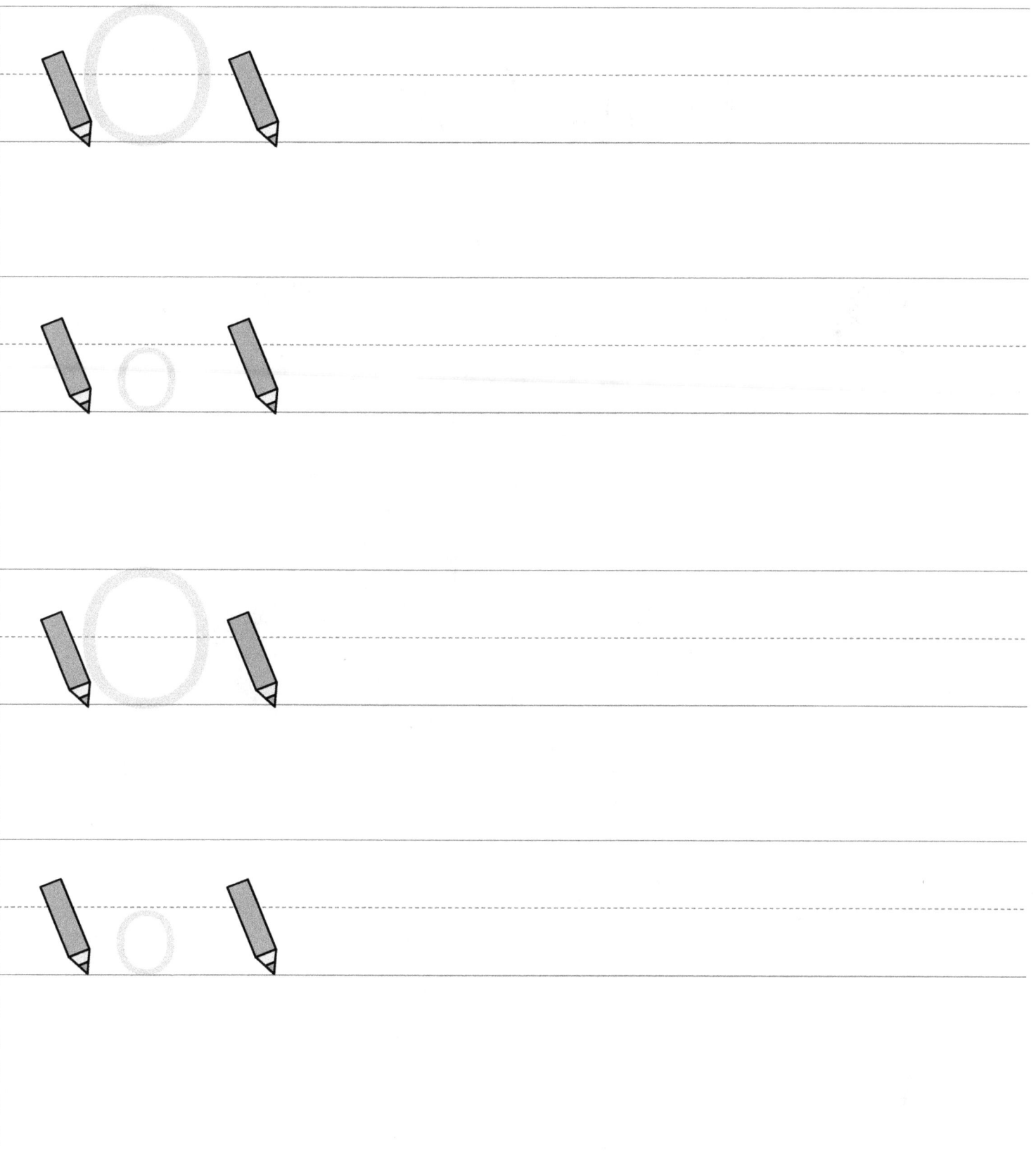

P is for...

Path

Q is for...

Quarry

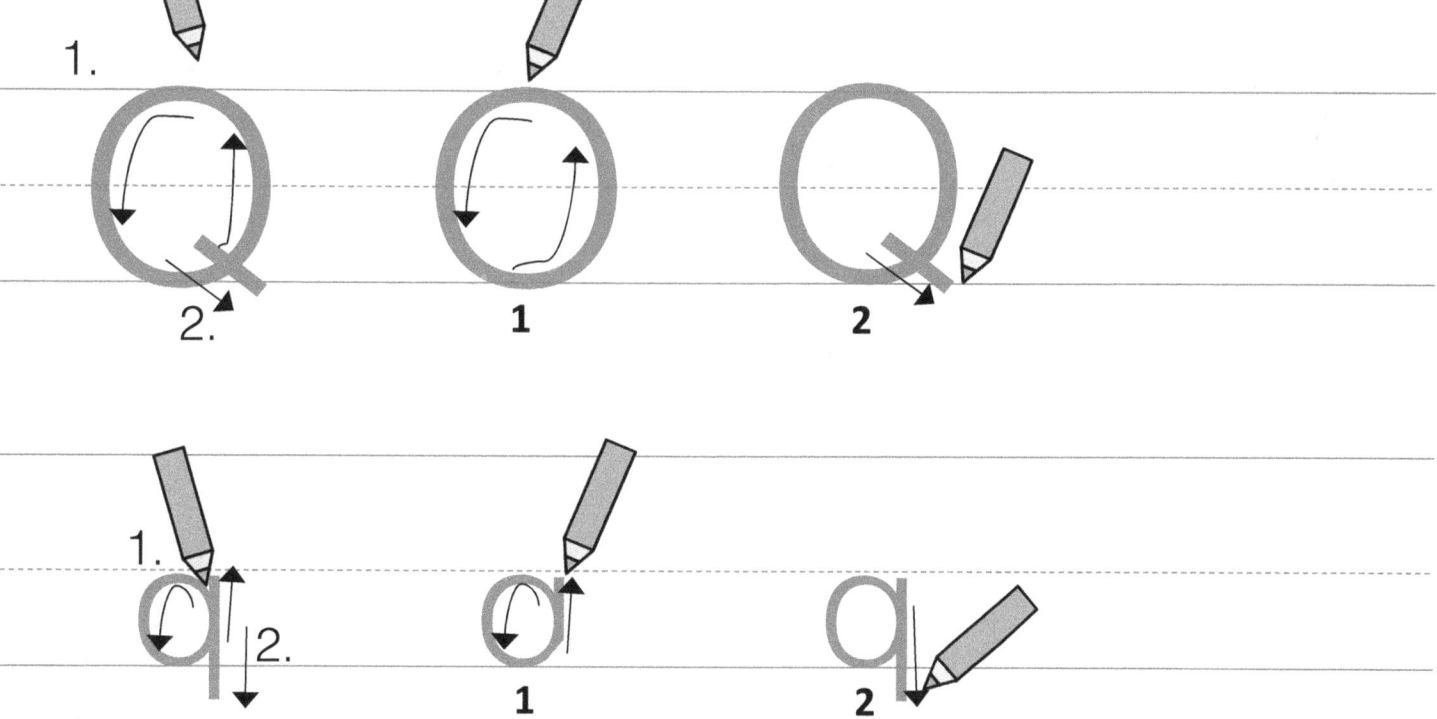

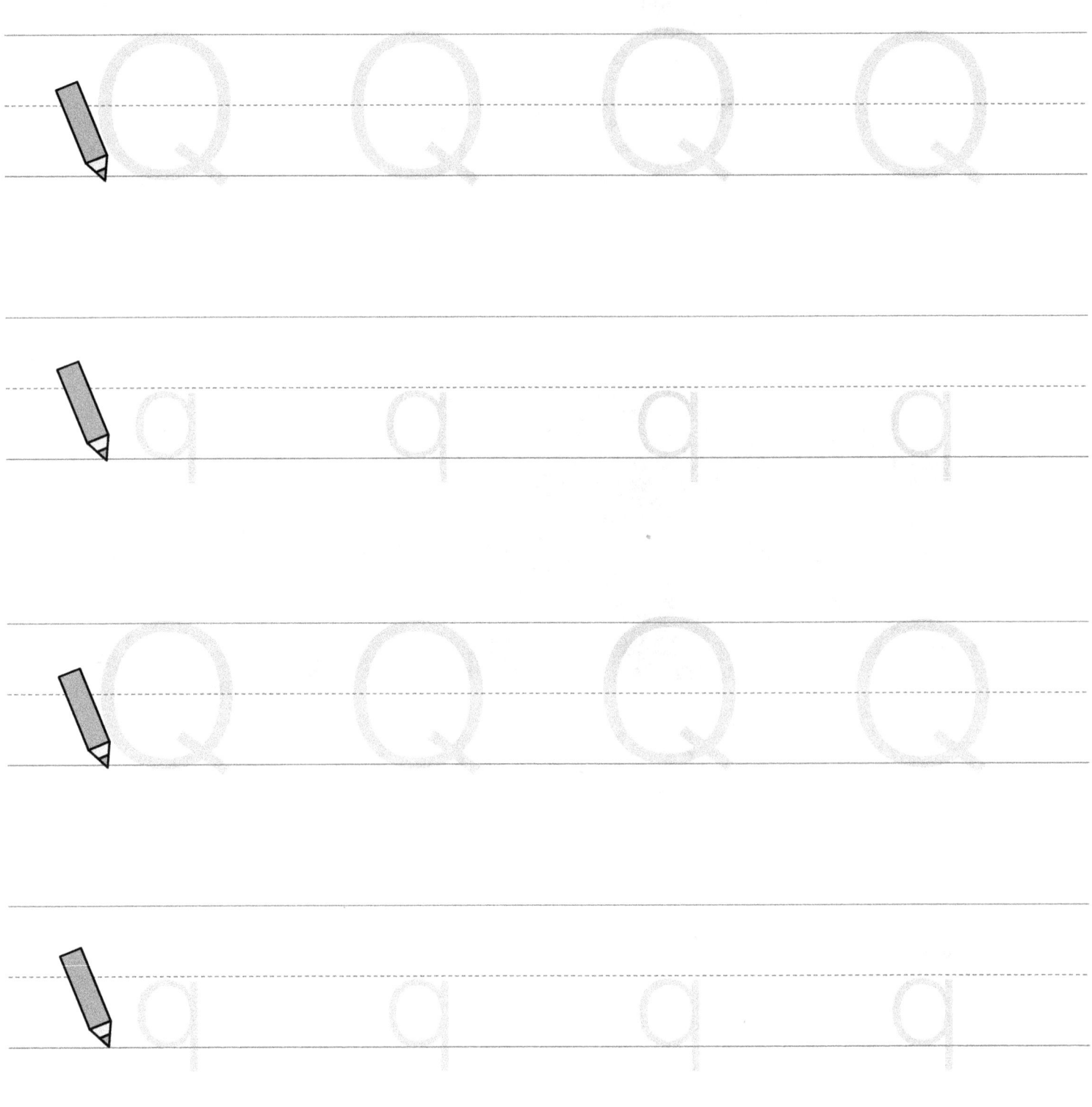

R is for...

River

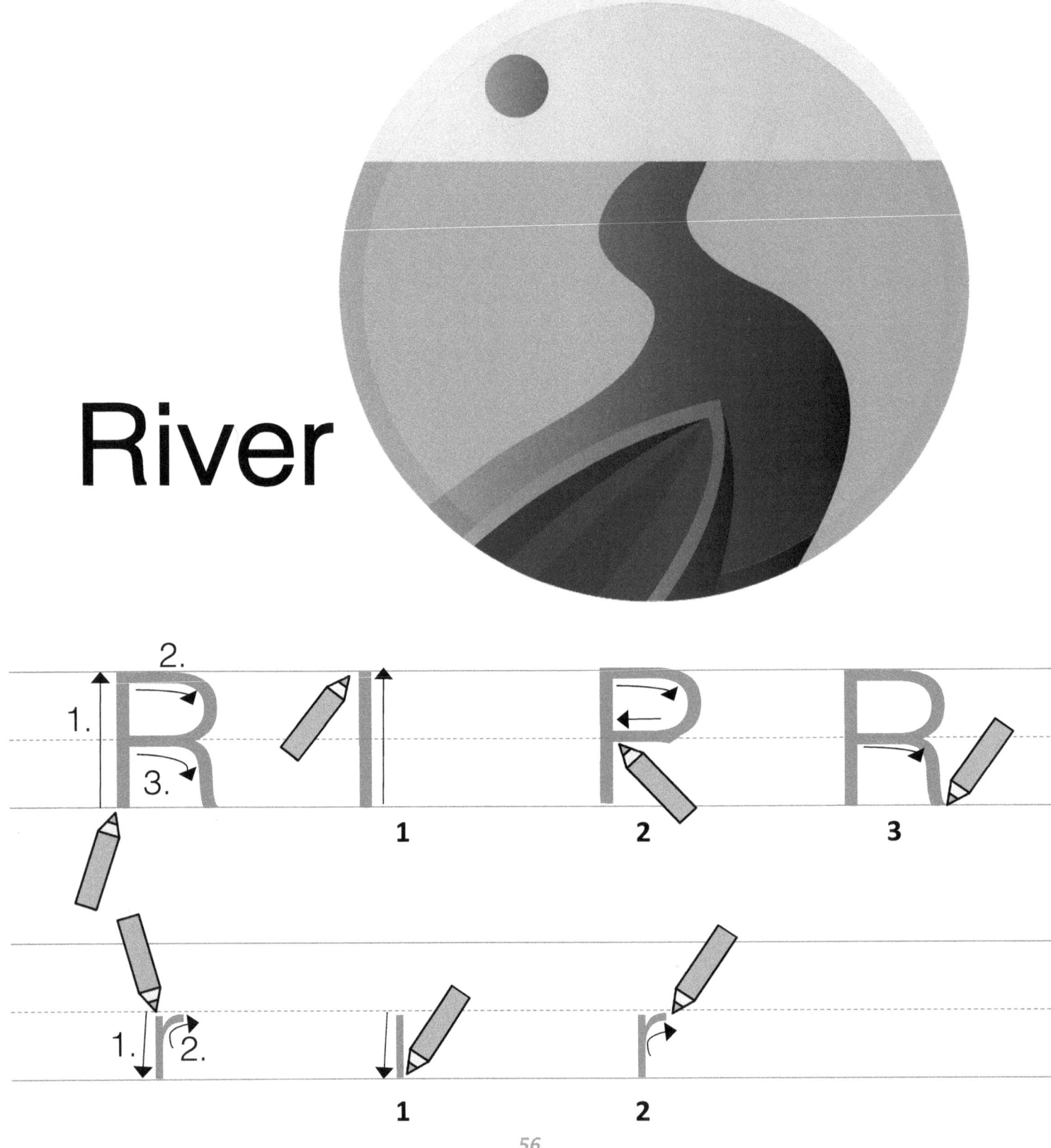

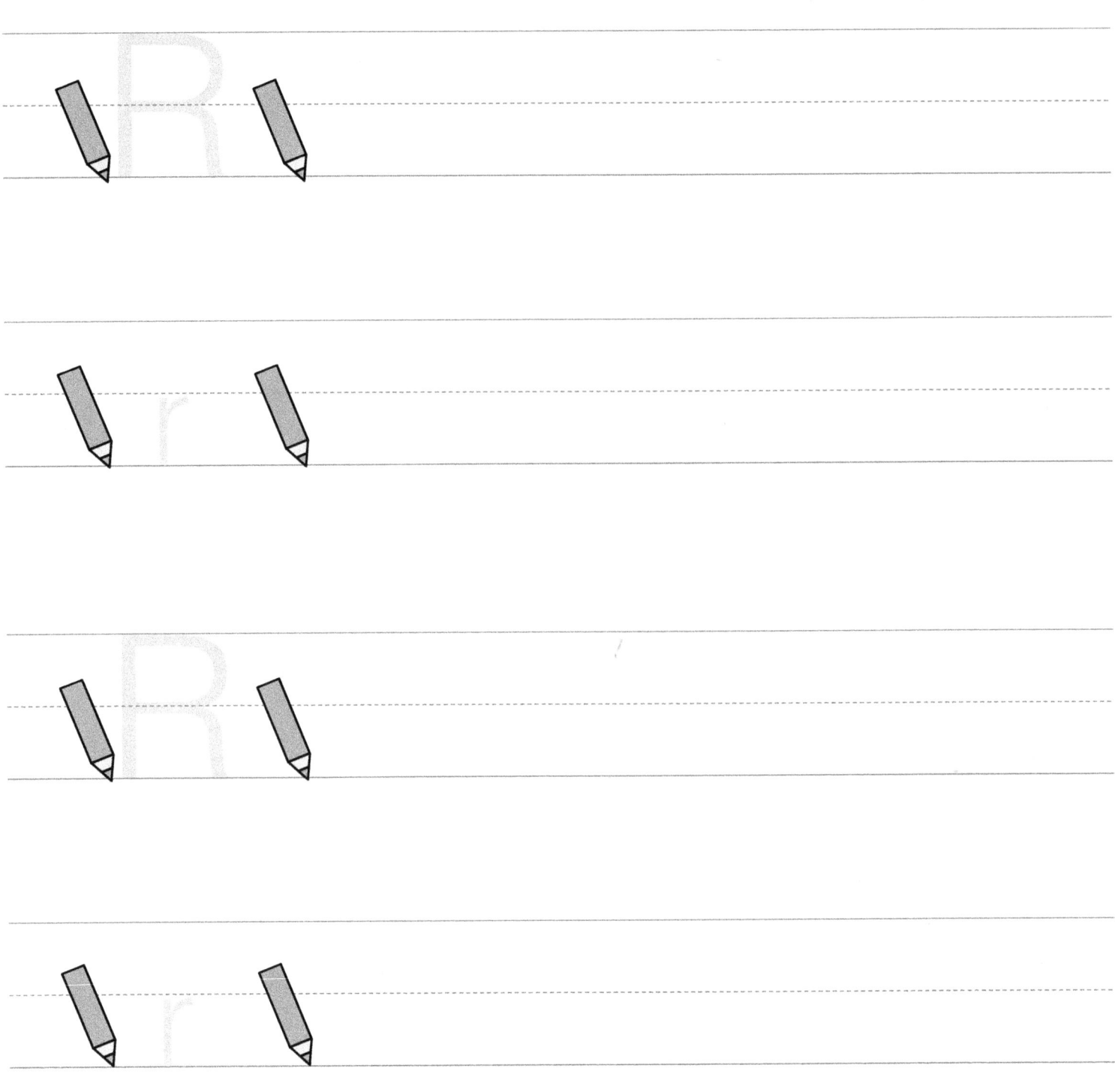

S is for...

Snow

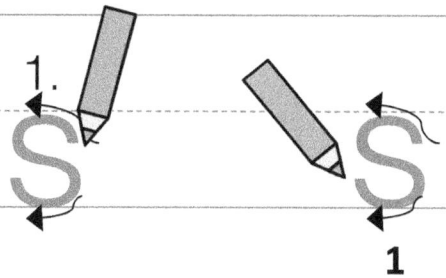

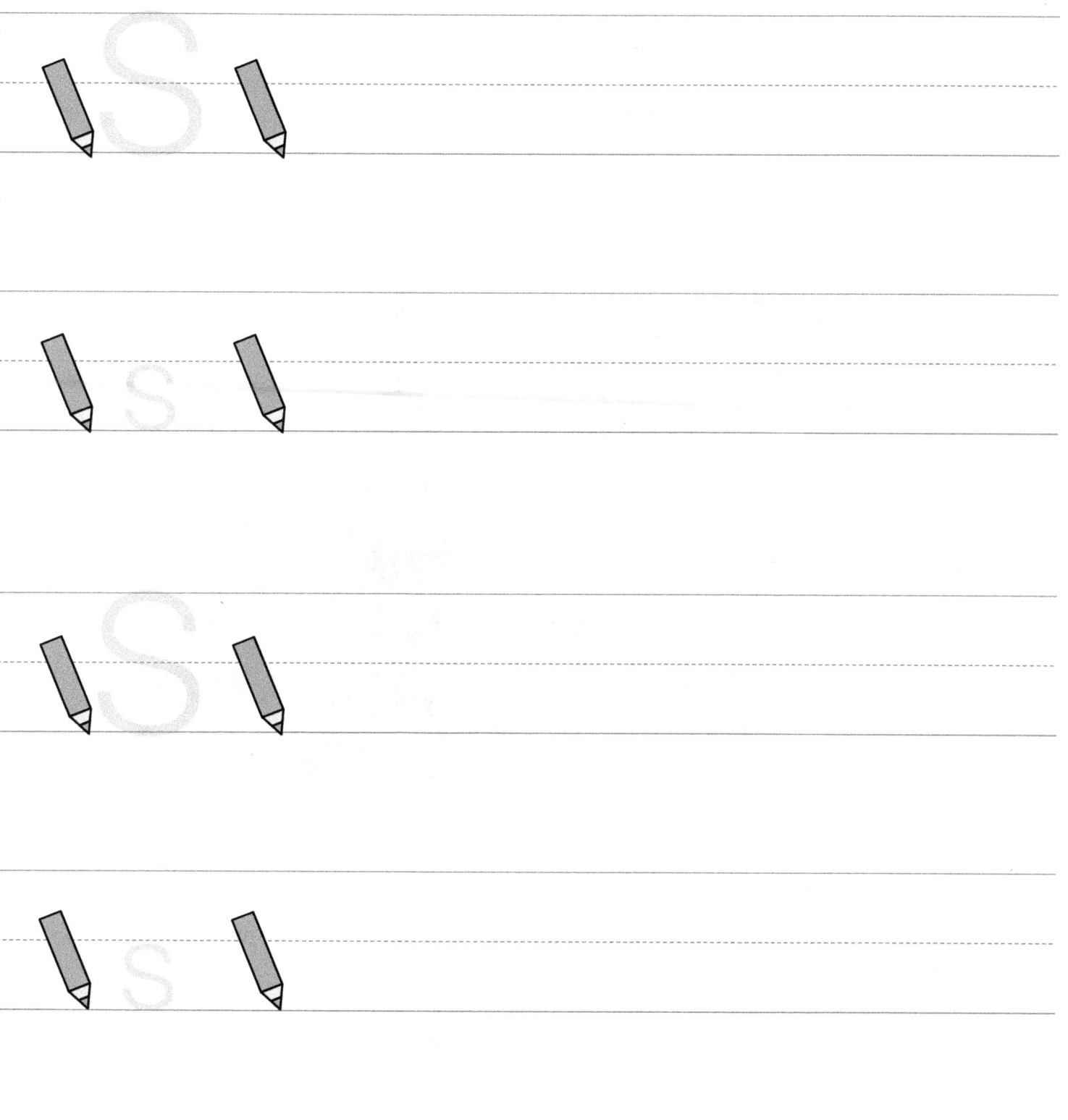

T is for…

Tent

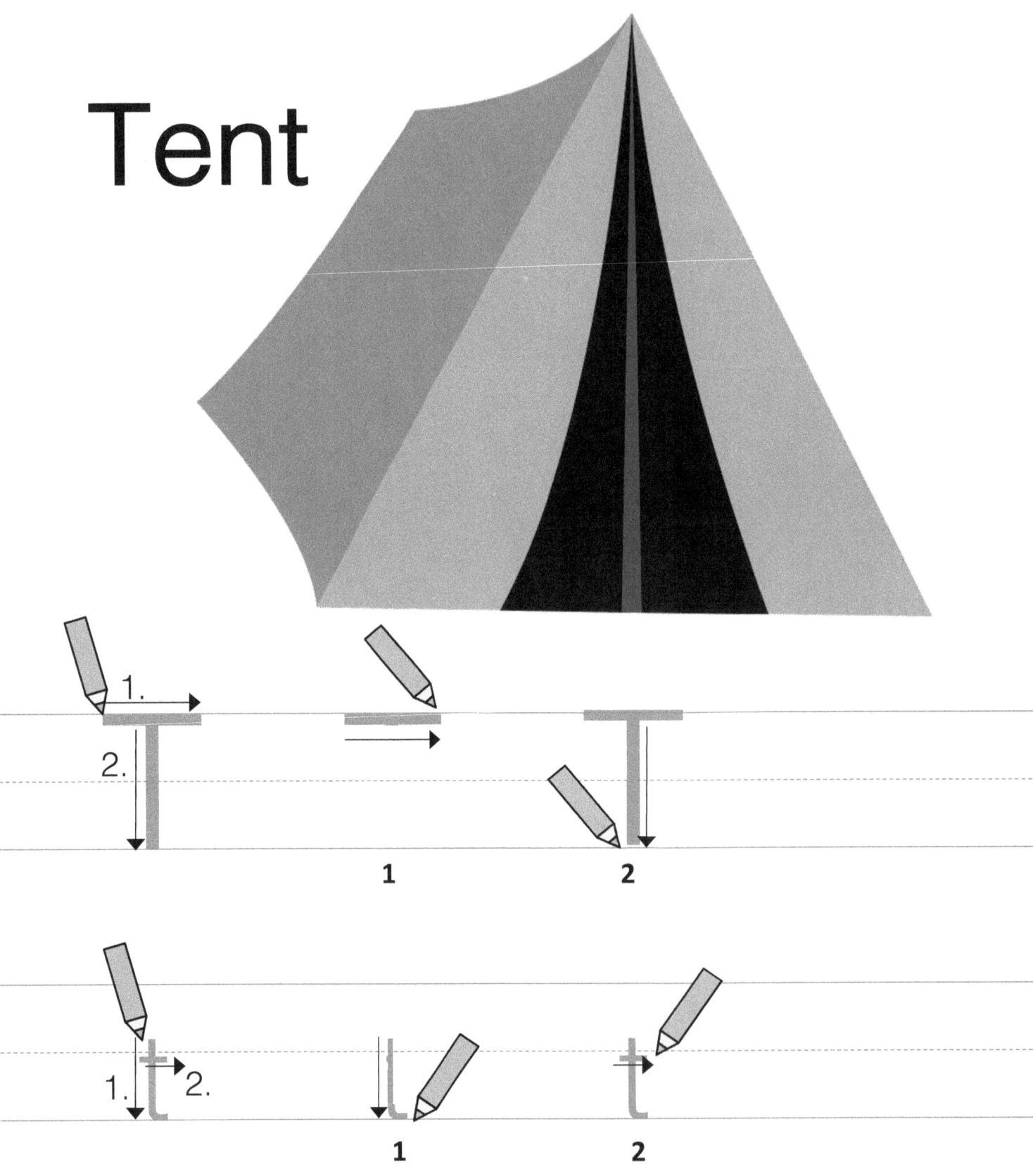

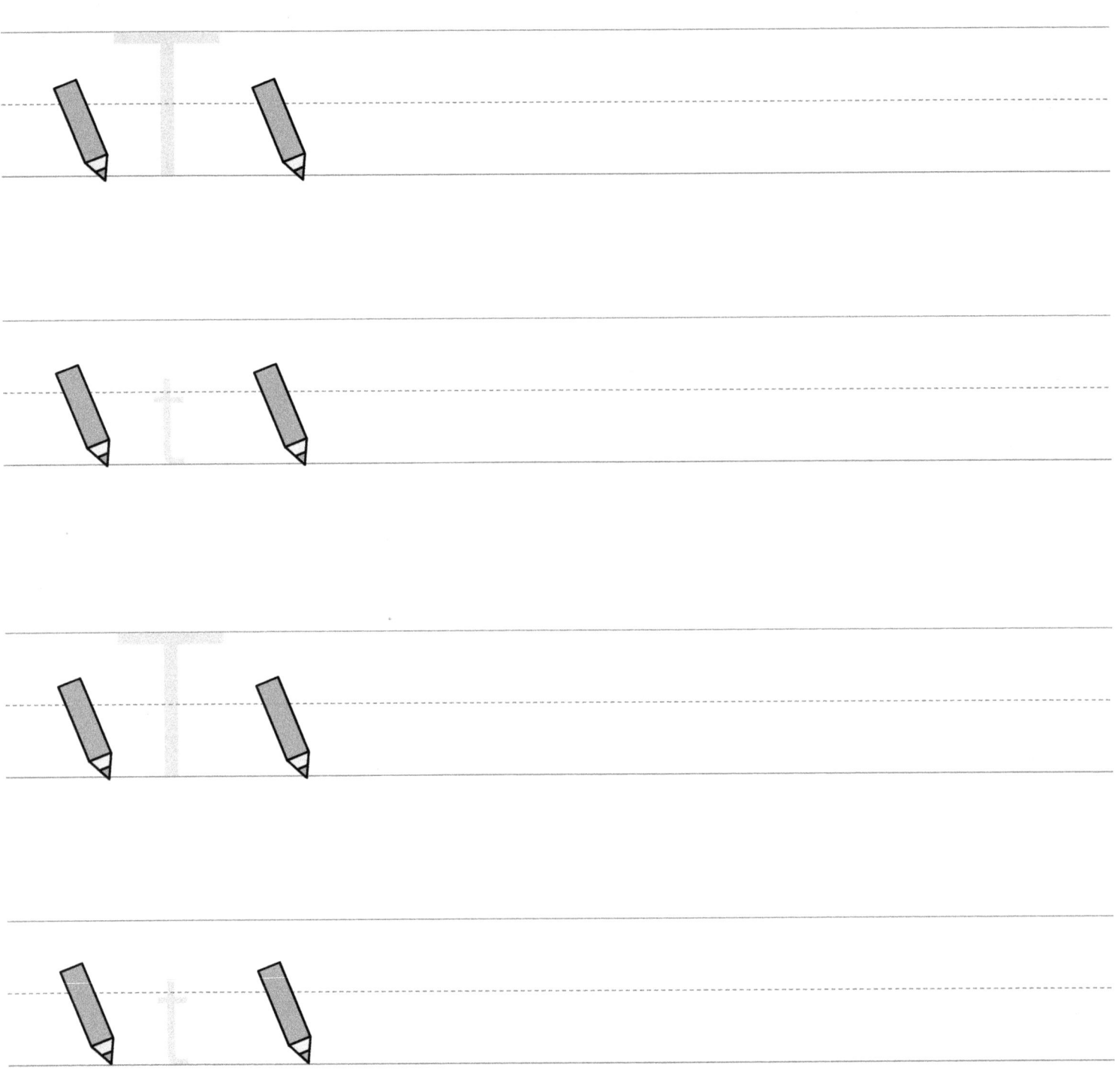

U is for...

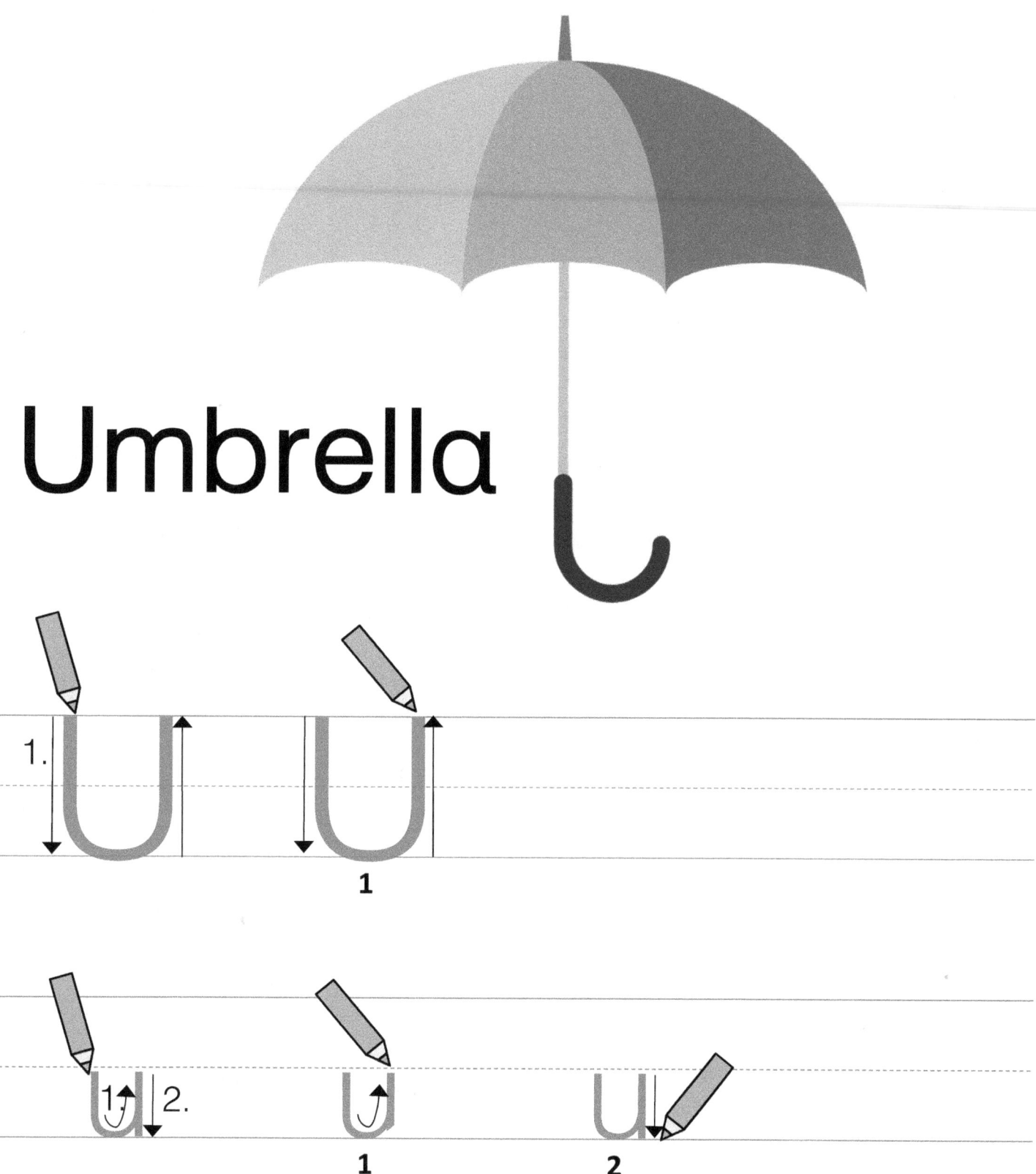

Umbrella

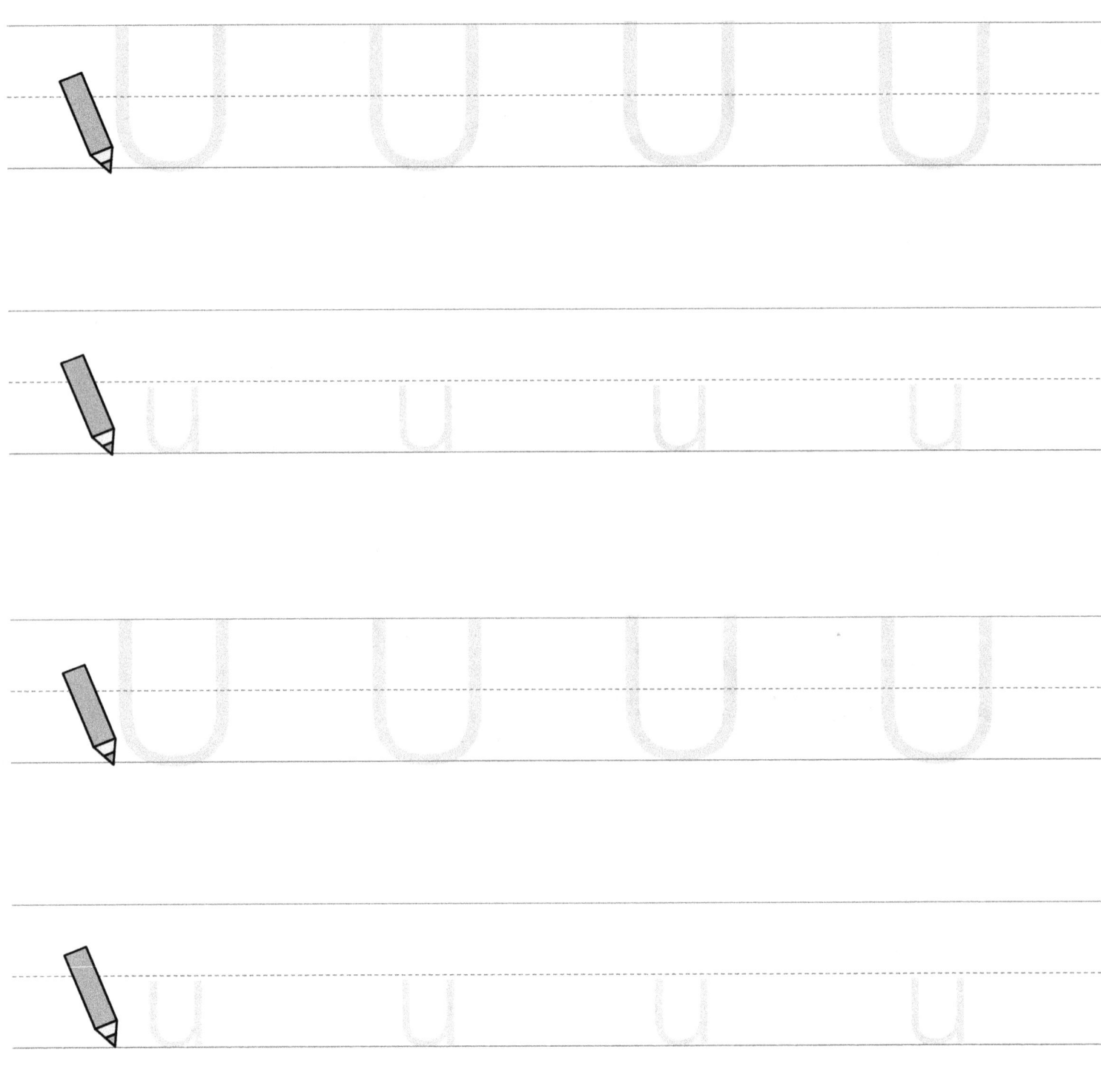

V is for...

Volcano

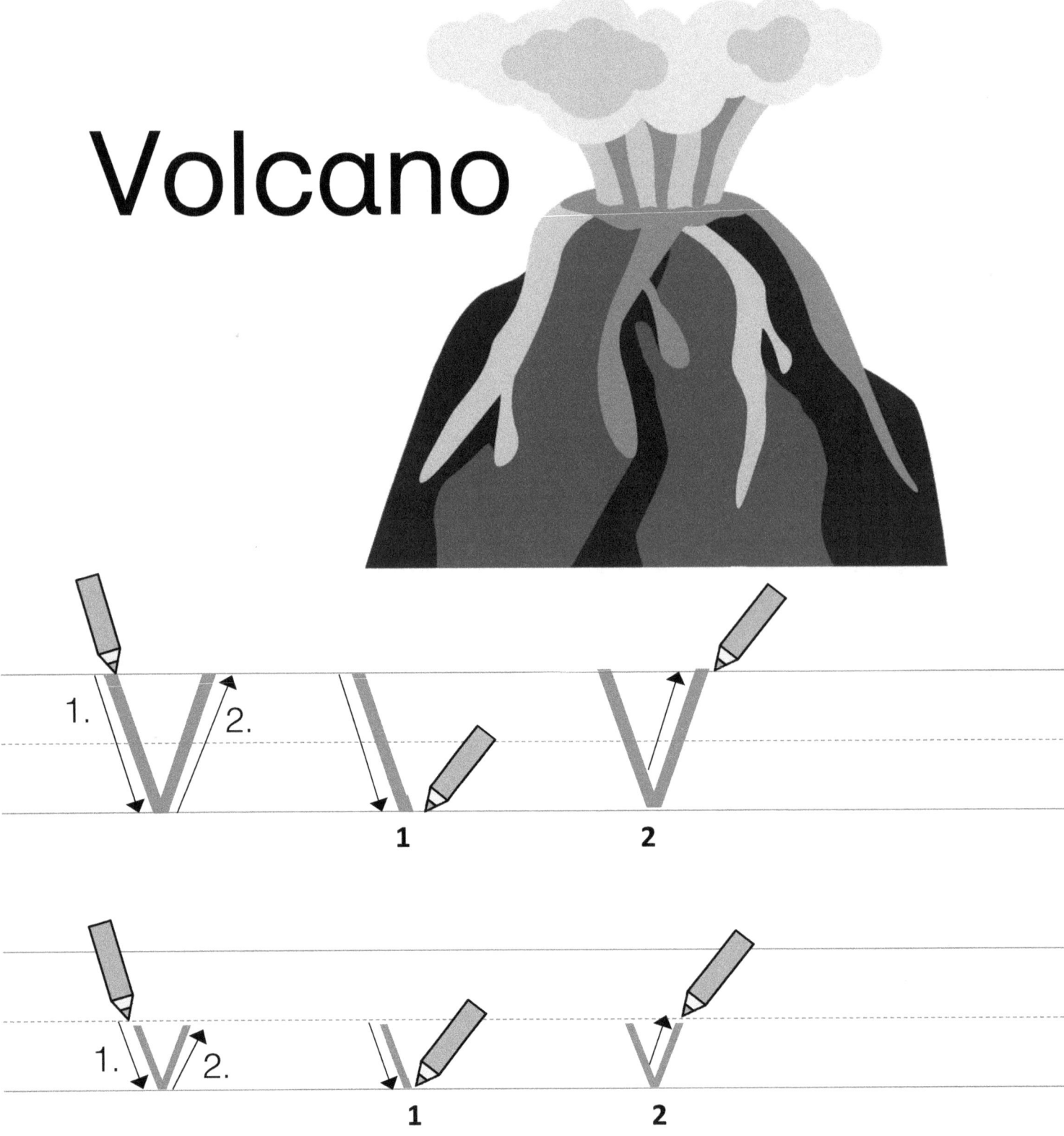

W is for...

Waterfall

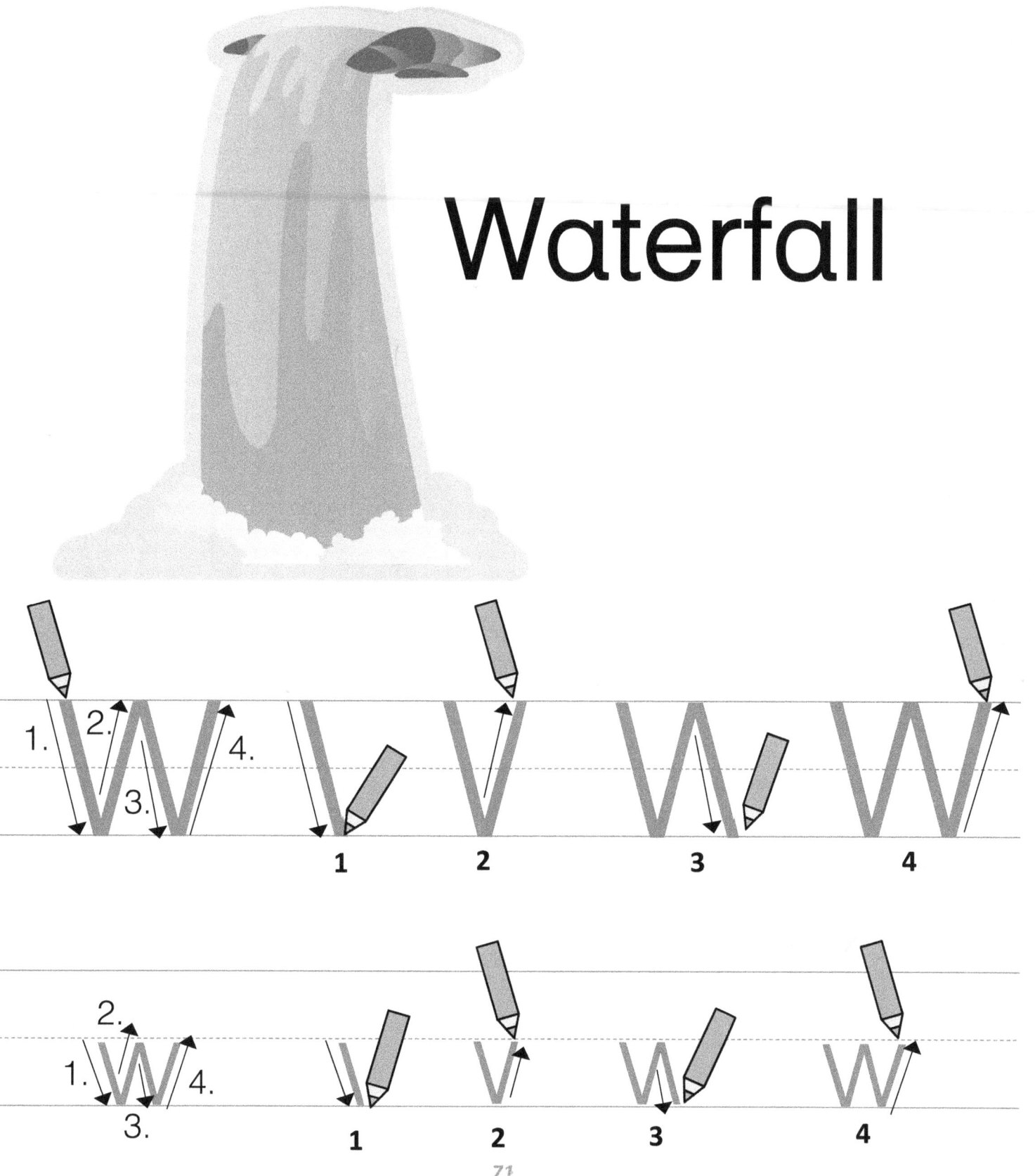

W W W W

W W W W

W W W W

W W W W

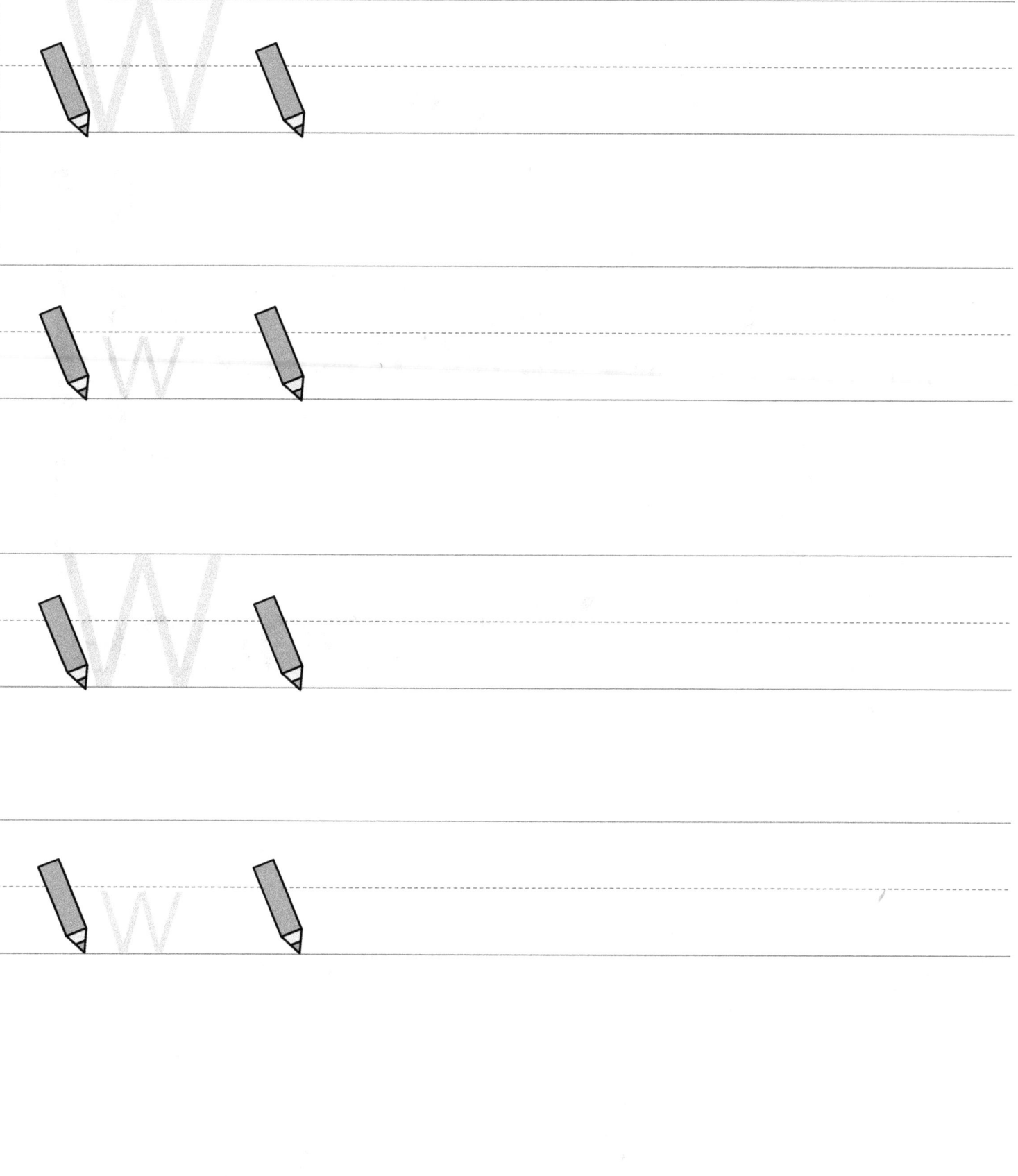

X is for...

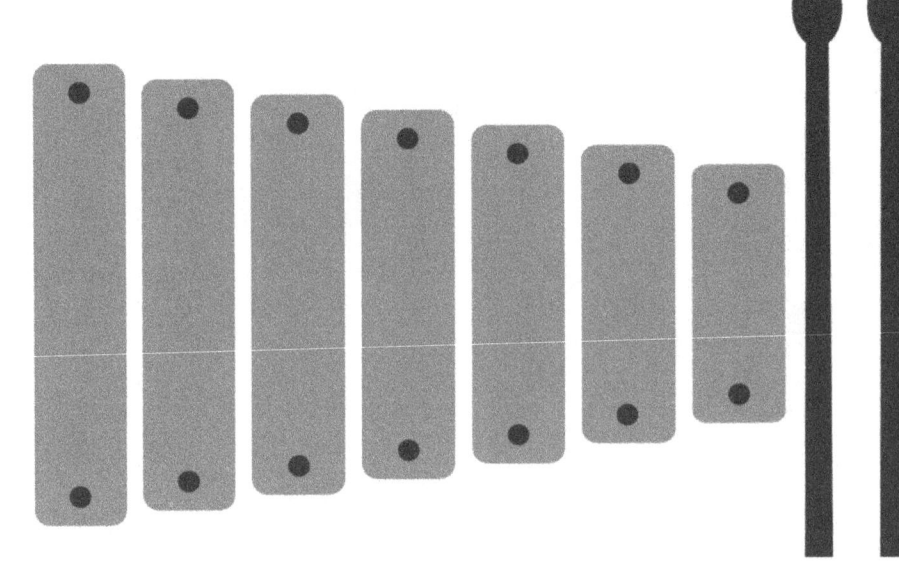

Xylophone

Not many words start with X, especially in nature, so we have used a musical instrument here!

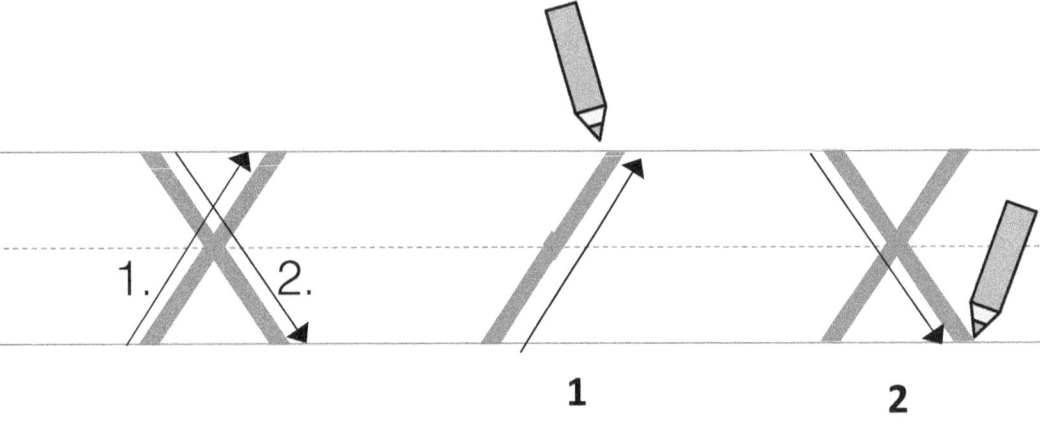

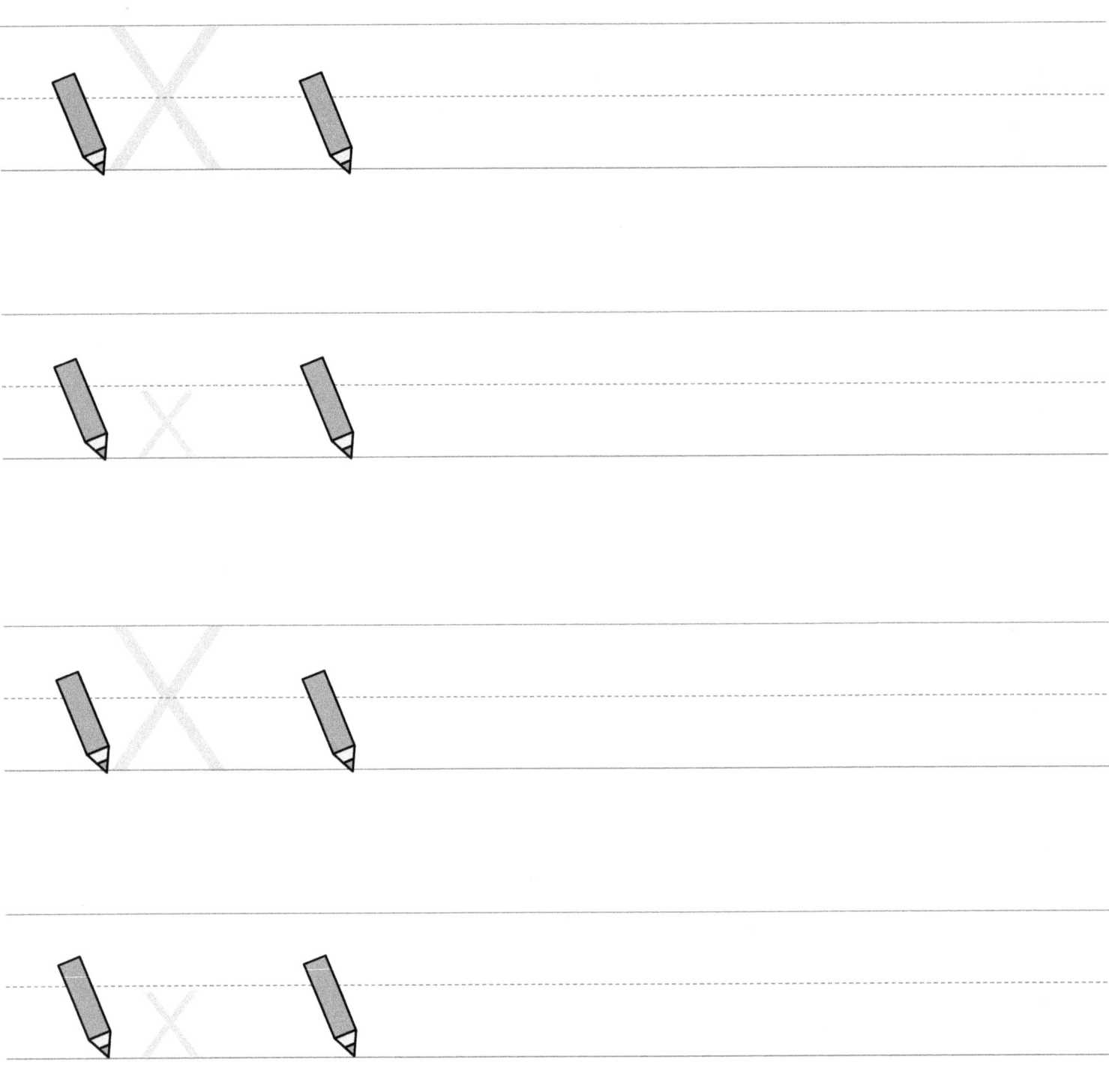

Y is for... Yak

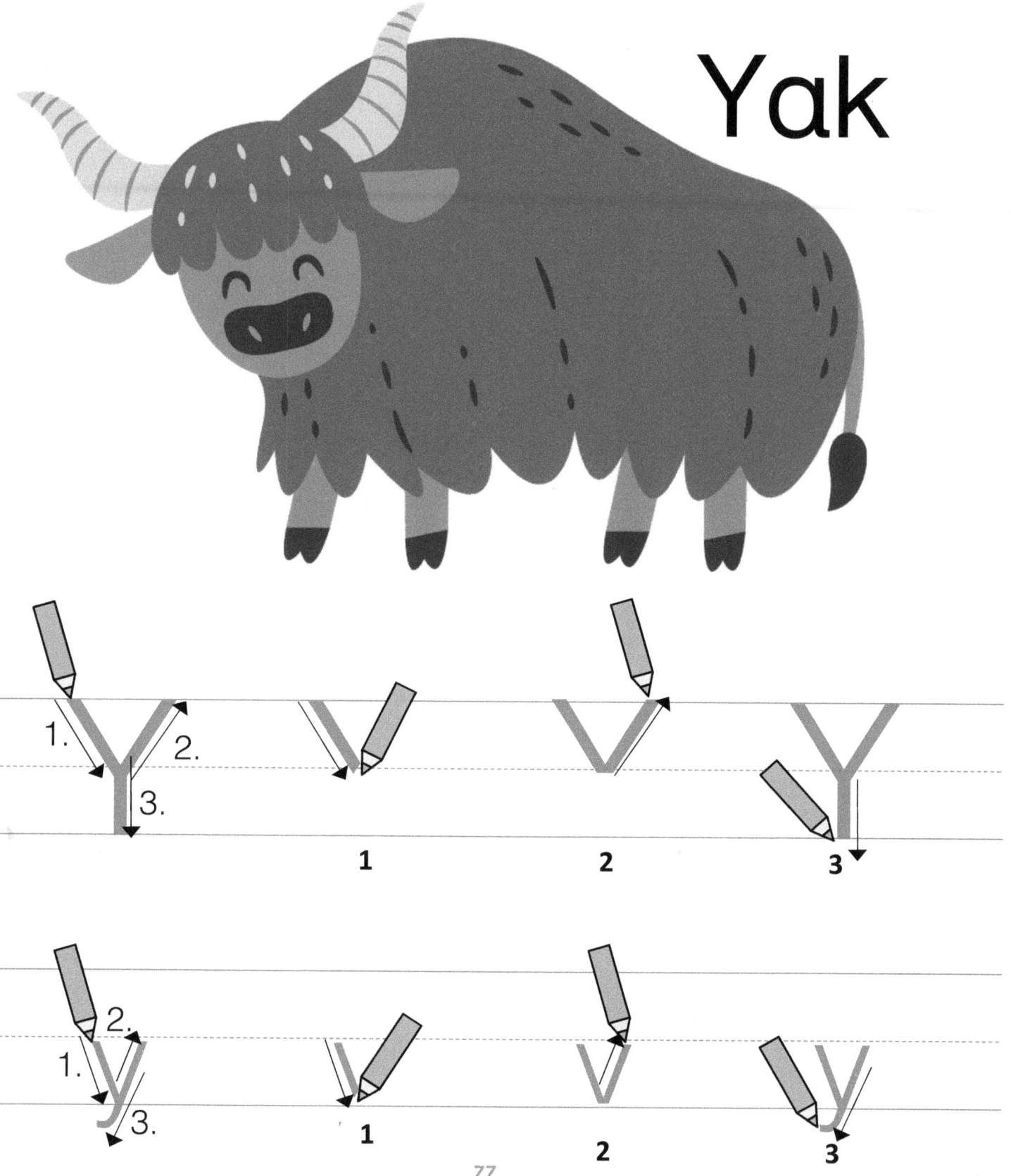

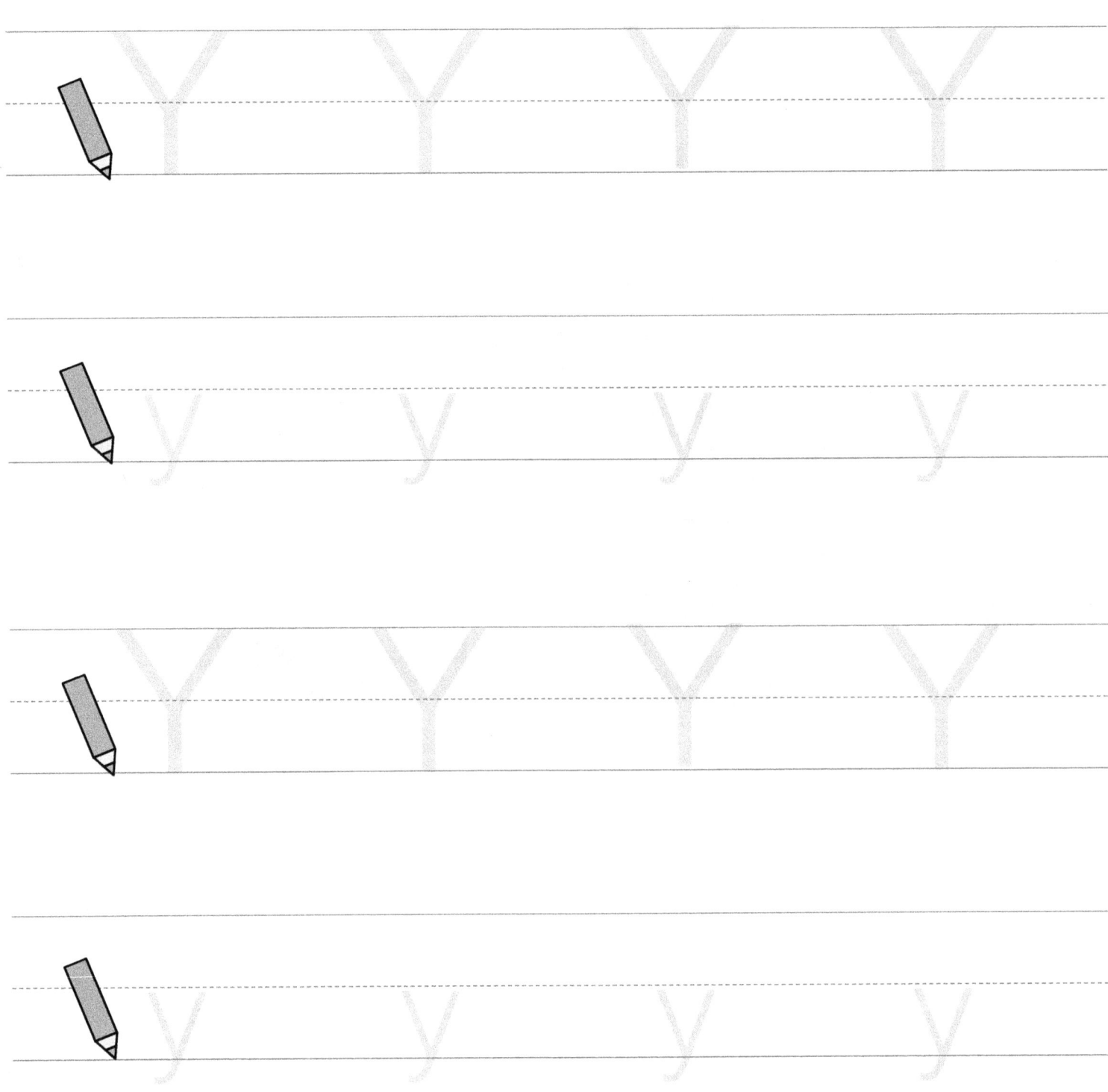

Z is for...

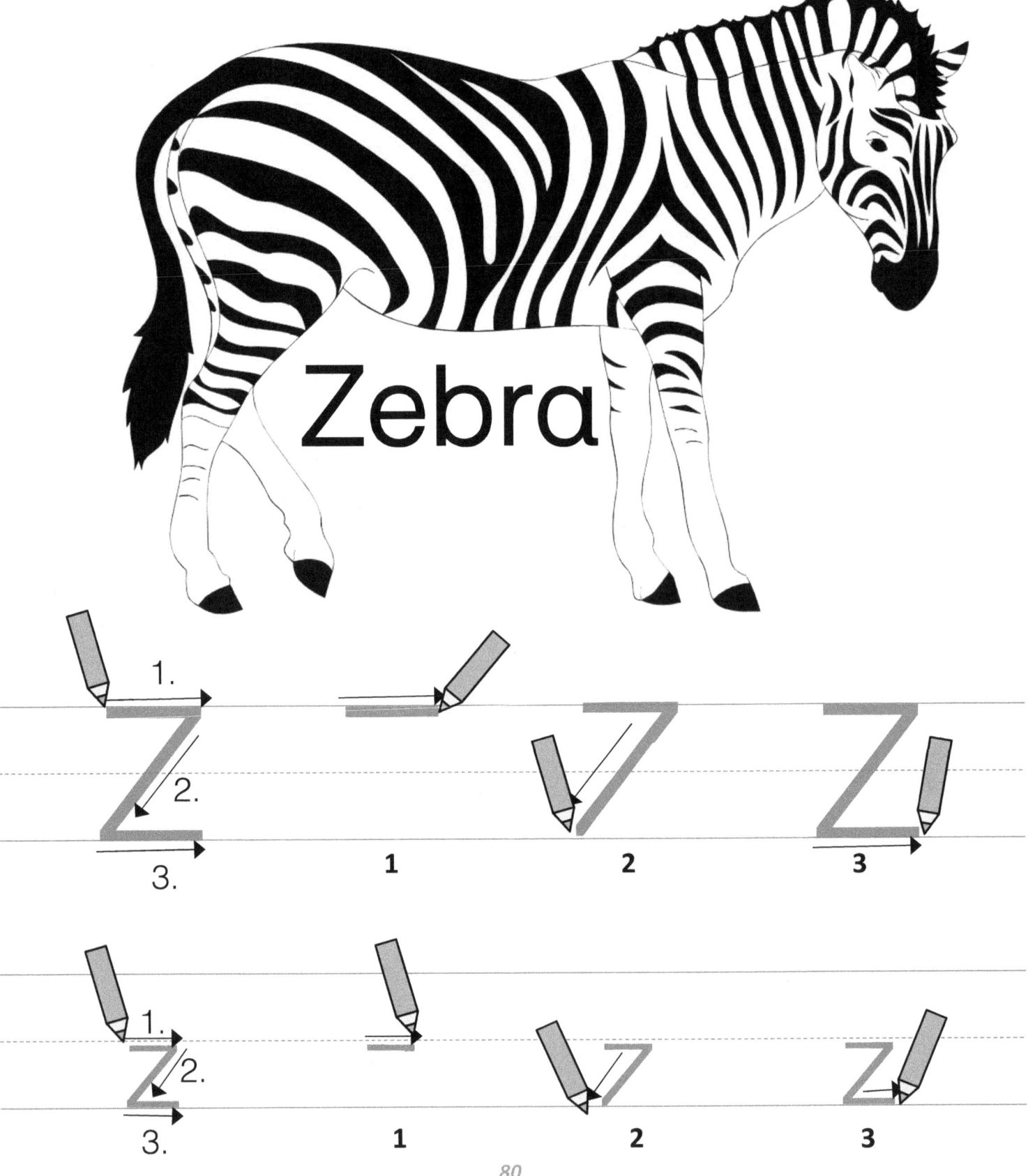

Zebra

Very well done for completing the letters. If you are feeling ready for a challenge, have a look to your right.

ZEBRA

To write a word, you just group letters together. If you have forgotten, just go back to the page! Here ZEBRA is all in capital letters, but that's not how we write a word!

zebra

Here, zebra is all in lowercase. This is fine if zebra is in the middle of a sentence, but to start a sentence, it must start with a capital letter, like shown below. Give it a try!

Zebra   Zebra

Zebra Zebra

Zebra Zebra

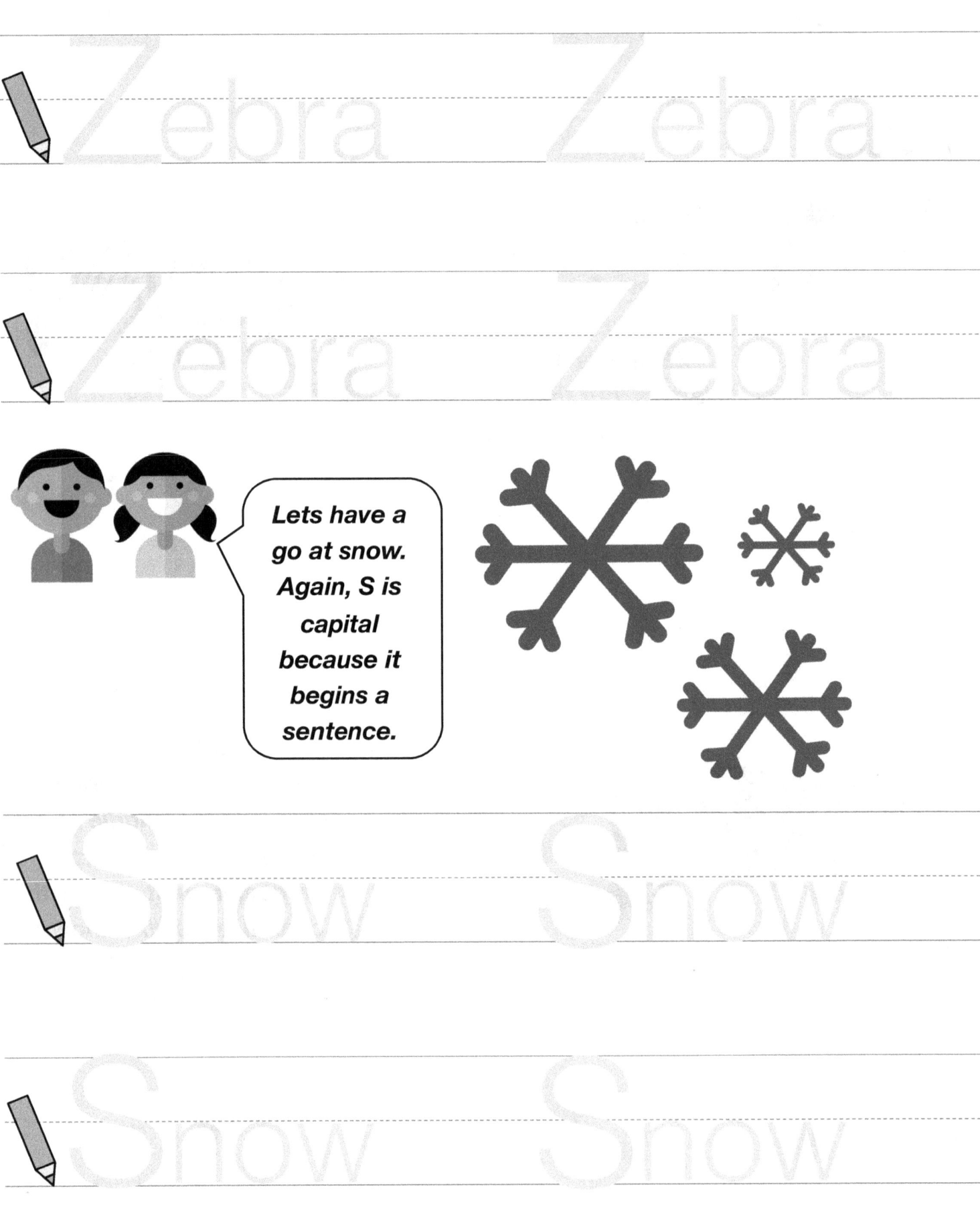
Lets have a go at snow. Again, S is capital because it begins a sentence.

Snow Snow

Snow Snow

snow snow

snow snow

Beach Beach

Beach Beach

beach   beach

beach   beach

Path   Path

Path   Path

path   path

path   path

Jungle   Jungle

Jungle   Jungle

jungle jungle

jungle jungle

Volcano Volcano

Volcano Volcano

volcano   volcano

volcano   volcano

Let's try our first sentence! It is exactly the same as you are doing with words, do not worry! We just leave a letter sized space between the words in a sentence.

I see a zebra.

I see a zebra.

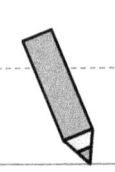 I see a zebra.

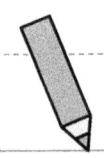 I see a zebra.

 *Remember at the end of every sentence, we use a full stop.*

 At the beach.

 At the beach.

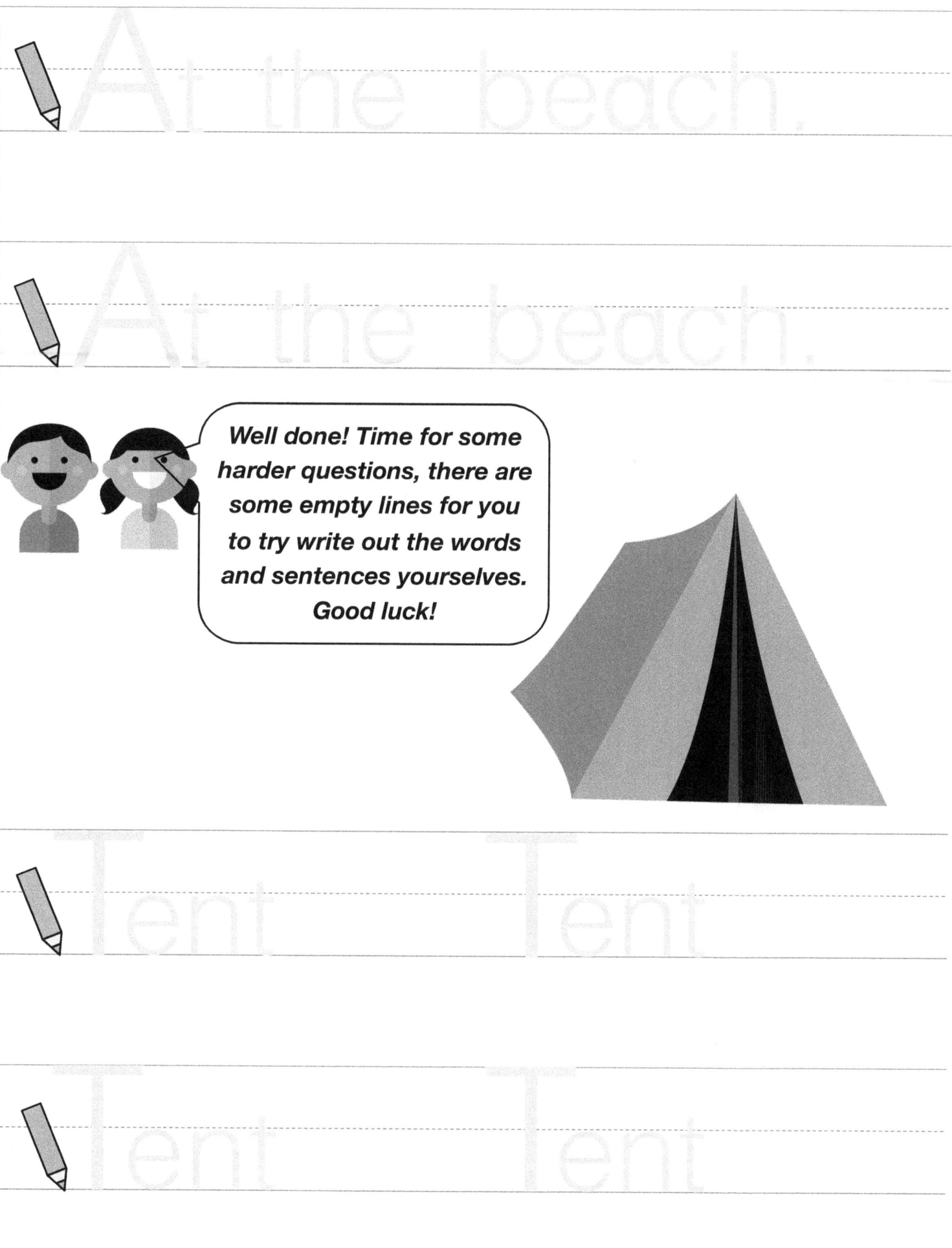

Desert   Desert

Desert   Desert

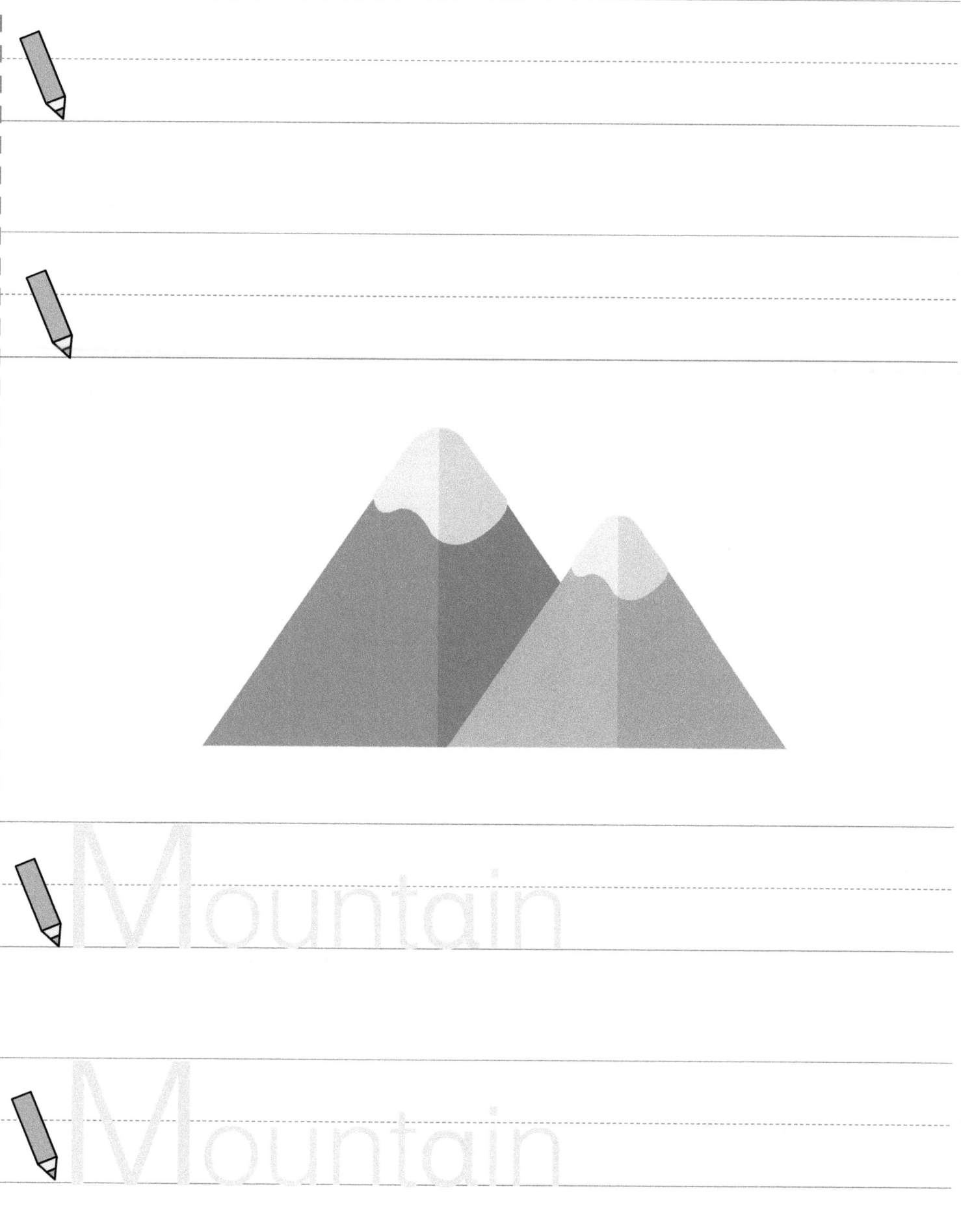

Mountain

Mountain

Waterfall

Waterfall

Island

Island

Nature   Lake

Nature   Lake

Nature   Lake

Nature   Lake

Umbrella Yak

Umbrella Yak

Umbrella Yak

Umbrella Yak

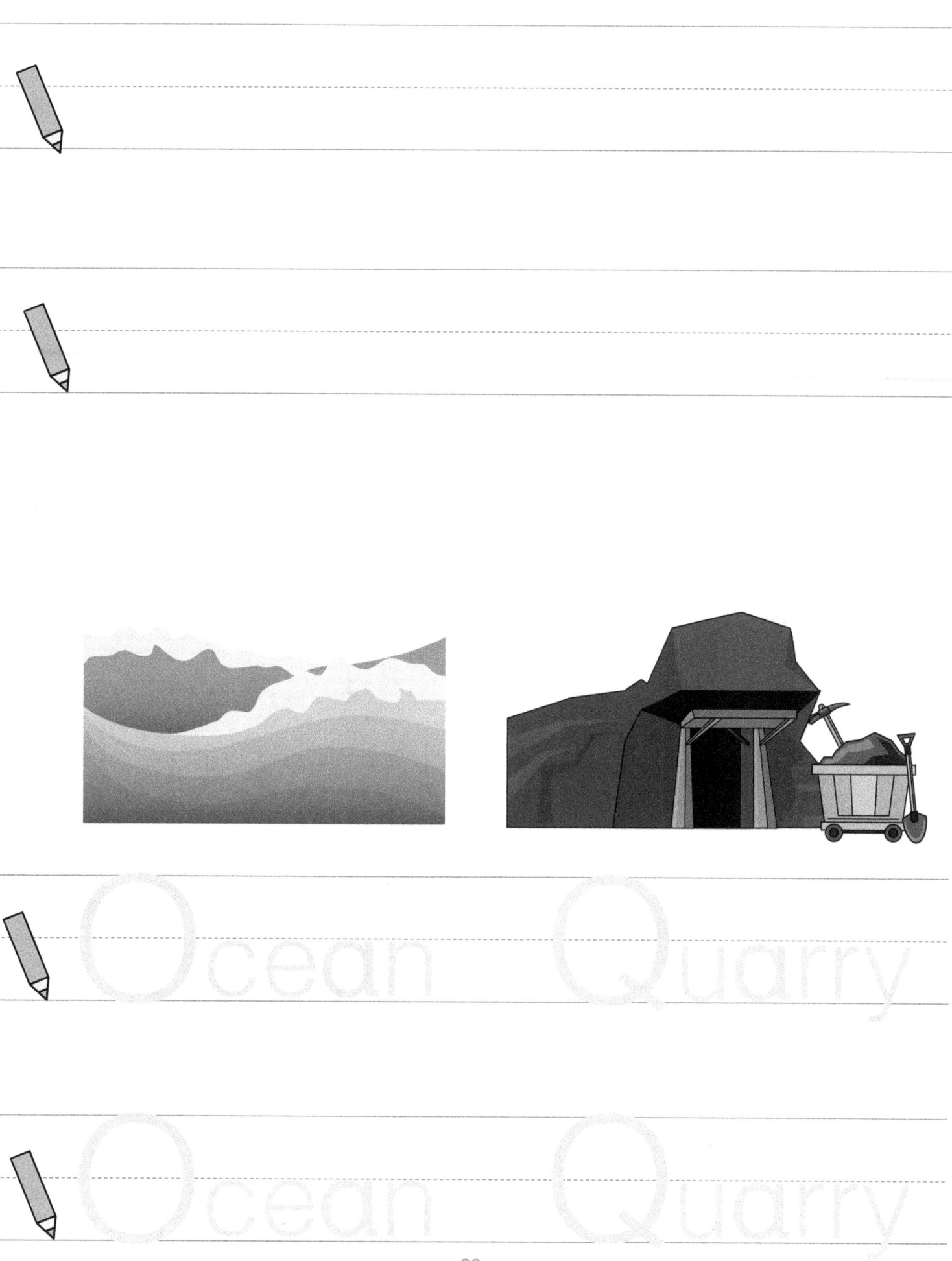

Ocean   Quarry

Ocean   Quarry

Desert   Earth

Desert   Earth

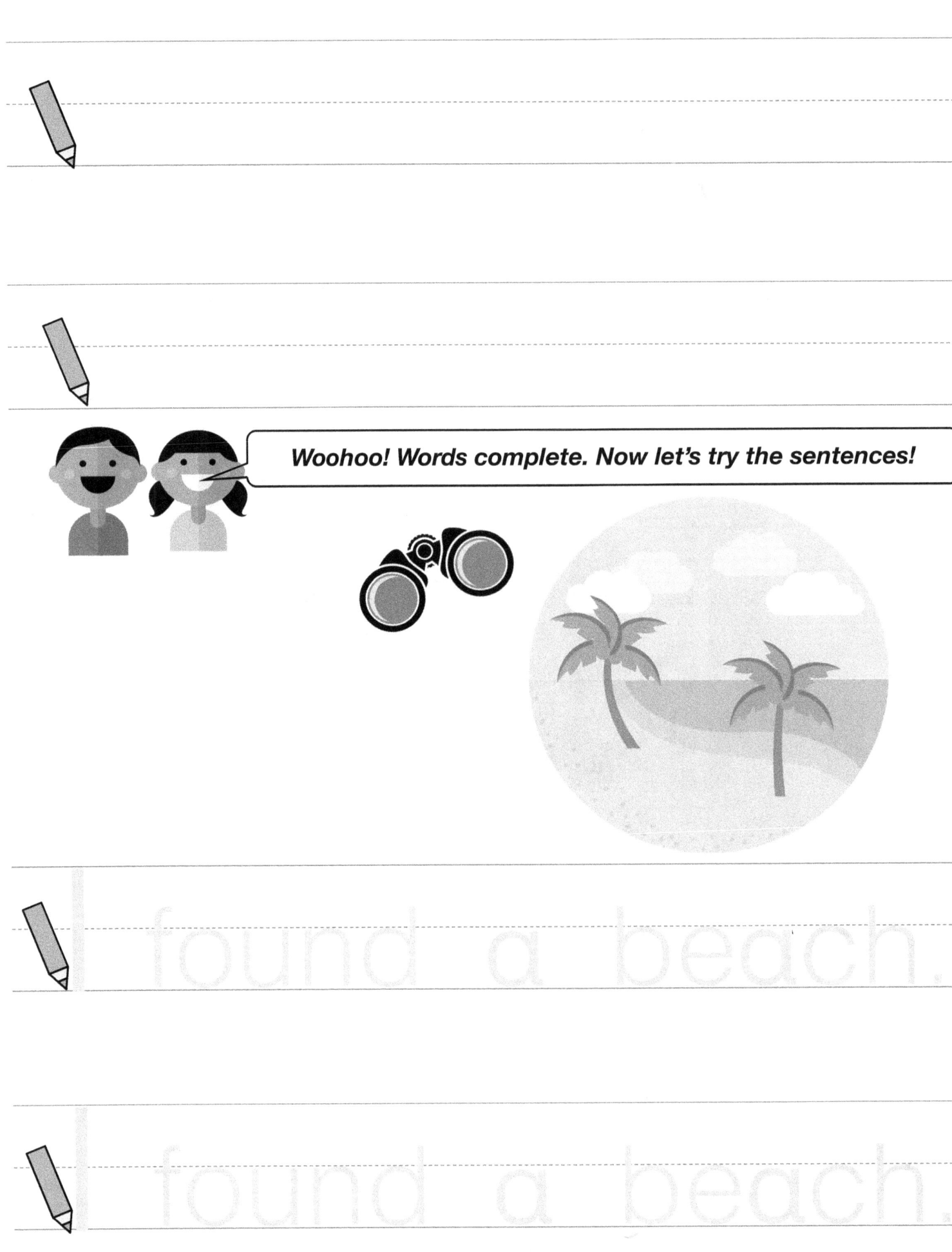

I found a beach.

I found a beach.

I found a beach.

Kangaroos hop.

Kangaroos hop.

Grass is green.

Grass is green.

Snow is cold.

Snow is cold.

I hid in a cave.

I hid in a cave.

Well done so far! The sentences are going to get harder, so get ready!

The path goes

into the forest.

The path goes

into the forest.

The river flows

into the ocean.

The river flows into the ocean.

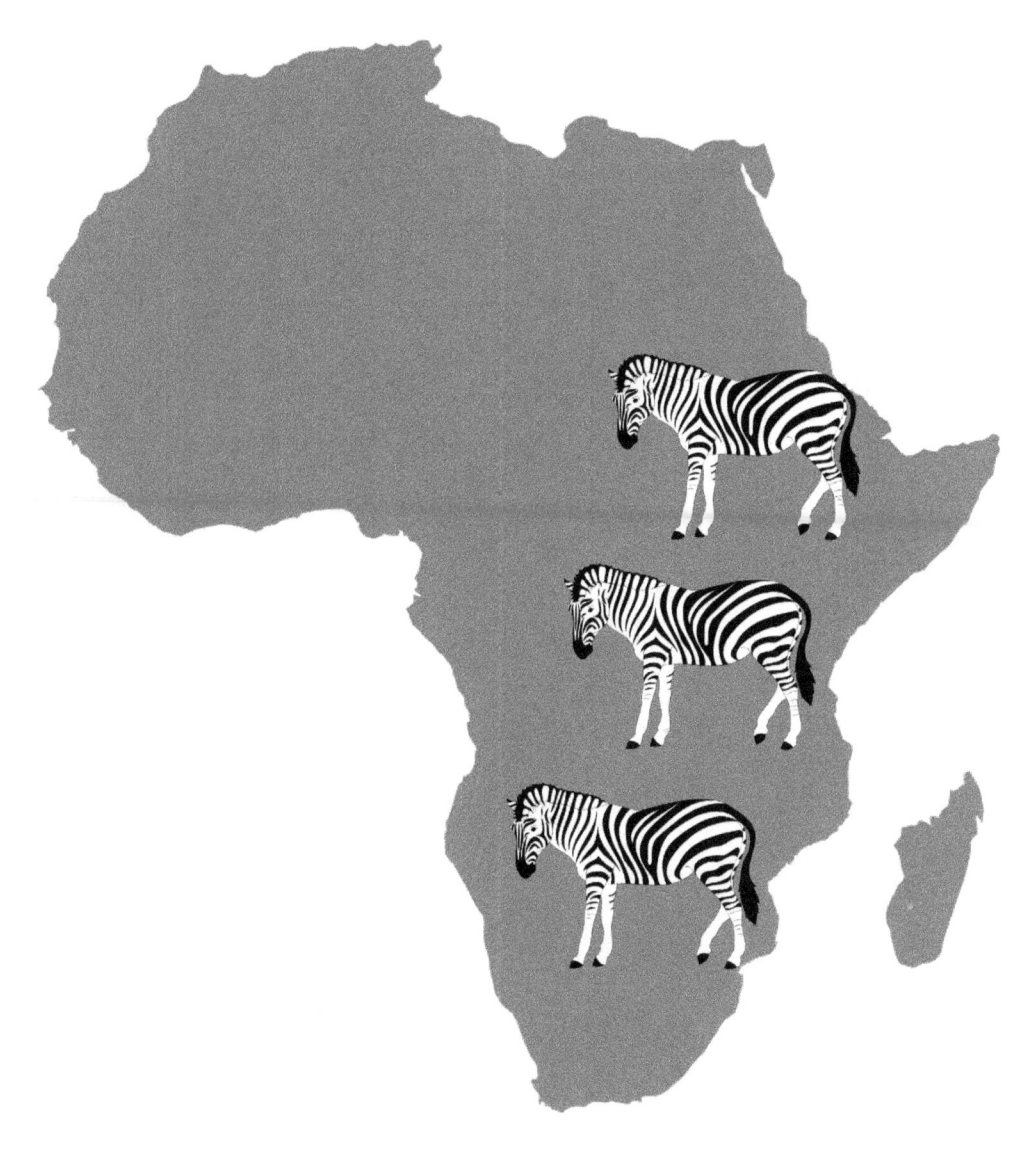

Zebras are found in Africa.

Zebras are

found in Africa.

There is a hut in the jungle.

There is a hut in

the jungle.

Waterfalls are part of nature.

Waterfalls are part of nature.

A very big well done for completing the questions. Give yourself a tap on the back, you deserve it! It took us longer than you did when we were kids to complete this. We have left you a few pages of blank handwriting guides to try a few letters, words or sentences yourselves.

www.ingramcontent.com/pod-product-compliance
Lightning Source LLC
Chambersburg PA
CBHW081015040426
42444CB00014B/3214